# Secrets of the Friendly Woods

Over the blurred alders hung the pale segment of a new April moon

CENTENNIAL EDITION

# SECRETS OF THE FRIENDLY WOODS


REX BRASHER

WITH ILLUSTRATIONS BY THE AUTHOR


FOREWORD BY
CYNTHIA CARTER AYRES, REX BRASHER ASSOCIATION


LP
LYONS PRESS

Essex, Connecticut

An imprint of The Globe Pequot Publishing Group, Inc.
64 South Main Street
Essex, CT 06426
www.globepequot.com


First edition published 1926 by The Century Co.



British Library Cataloguing in Publication Information available

Library of Congress Cataloging-in-Publication Data available

ISBN 978-1-4930-9777-7 (paperback)
ISBN 978-1-4930-9851-4 (ebook)

To the birds of
Chickadee Valley—
Their friends and ours.

# CONTENTS

# ILLUSTRATIONS

# Illustrations

## Illustrations

# FOREWORD

WHO was Rex Brasher?

Born in 1869 in Brooklyn, he witnessed the opening of the Brooklyn Bridge and the unveiling of the Statue of Liberty. He liked to think his ancestors were pirates. As a boy, he shot birds, but as a man, he deeply regretted taking those lives. He traveled the country on foot and by boat as the nineteenth century ended, spending hours silently studying living birds as they went about their business. He spent most of his long life in the twentieth century, living in the woods, often alone but never friendless. He quietly painted every kind of bird in North America in its natural habitat. When Rex died in 1960, the *New York Herald Tribune* carried an extensive obituary, "Rex Brasher Is

Dead: Renowned Bird Painter," with this apt description: "In pursuit of his elusive quarry, Mr. Brasher probably spent more time in trees, behind brambles, or crouched in a duck boat than most men spend at the office."

After completing his last painting in 1924, Rex believed his greatest adventure would be "finished when all the little feathered fellows were portrayed on paper and snugly stowed away in a fireproof safe." So, he sat down to write *Secrets of the Friendly Woods*. In this entertaining and enlightening little book, he reflected on his experiences in the woods (and on the water) and on some of his adventures along the way. Whether tracking a hairy woodpecker for hours while it hunted for grubs, saving an osprey from drowning, rescuing grouse eggs while fighting a forest fire, or describing the bloodthirstiness of the goshawk, Rex wrote with humor and conviction.

A reviewer in the *Springfield Republican* described *Secrets of the Friendly Woods* as "intimate in detail," showing "a love for wild life that carries conviction. His contact with wild life is presented with an evident desire to see it protected and continued that it may be enjoyed."

If Rex had a religion besides the Golden Rule, it was his devotion to the beauty and wonder of the natural world. He fervently believed that human beings could learn a great deal from other creatures and from the forces of nature. Rex despised the use of traps and "the indifference of those who adorn themselves in furs of slaughtered wild folk."

Based on his many years of observing birds and other animals in the wild, Rex had serious reservations about the existence of divinity and even more about man's tendency toward destruction. "The feverish restlessness permeating the world today would disappear if we could emulate the simplicity and straightforward lives of the woods people. . . . We are learning. But a long interval of destruction may intervene."

Rex identified himself as a bird painter, but he was also a naturalist and an environmentalist. He often lamented the effects of human activity on bird species and their habitat. He wanted to believe that "consideration for all forms of wild life is gradually extending toward the high plane it eventually will obtain in man's evolution."

Rex recorded many of the threats facing birds. In 1930 he wrote that passenger pigeons had been spotted in Michigan. "But the millions which once darkened the sky with their moving thunder are as last year's appleblossoms; yet we do not seem to have learned much from this tragedy.—Seven and one half million 'sportsmen' are doing their best to send the rest of our birds and animals down the same trail." And he was dismayed by the approaching extinction of "the largest of our birds," the California vulture.

Rex was critical of the farmers who were destroying the California quail "because they eat a little grain or a few grapes . . . forgetting the thousands of injurious insects which they eliminate." He feared that the prairie chicken was "on the way to join the rapidly increasing members of birds which are only a memory" because their habitat was being cleared for wheat farms.

Rex did give credit to "enlightened farmers" for protecting the marsh hawk, which could "destroy nearly one thousand field mice in a season and save many a tree in a young orchard." And he applauded the success of government efforts to reverse the effects of man on declining bird populations, such as the federal migratory law that had given some respite to the band-tailed pigeon, which was nearing extinction. Rex particularly appreciated the protected status of the osprey throughout the eastern United States: "Any form of life that has obedient and well-behaved children deserves not only protection but all other praise imaginable!"

But Rex did not romanticize. "Nature is an impartial old dame, sometimes assisting the helpless, sometimes forgetting entirely and offering them up as a sacrifice to any rapacious pursuer which needs a meal." Describing how a Cooper's hawk gruesomely dismembered a young chicken, Rex managed to insert a sly reference to the Scopes trial (which dominated the news in July 1925).

Having become a farmer of sorts in the middle of his life, he soon learned hard truths. "That little cleared oasis isn't a garden, it's a battlefield, and every spring hostilities are renewed." Despite his epic attempts to thwart a resident woodchuck's decimation of his vegetable garden, Rex felt a certain degree of admiration for the stout fellow's tunnel construction, conceding that the woodchuck was the only animal in North America to have a day named after it.

When Rex published *Secrets of the Friendly Woods*, he thought he had finished his life's work. We have no way of knowing for sure, but it seems likely that the success of this little book inspired him to self-publish his twelve-volume

*Birds and Trees of North America*, which not only reproduced the paintings but also added accompanying descriptive text for each species. The overwhelmingly positive reception of that work certainly contributed to his determination to find a permanent home for the paintings. When Rex died, he believed that he had succeeded.

You might be wondering why you've never heard of Rex Brasher. The story begins with Rex's father, Philip, an amateur ornithologist who donated his collection of specimens to Yale University. As a child, Rex spent hours with his father exploring the woods and waterways surrounding Brooklyn, searching out and identifying birds.

Perhaps because Philip died when Rex was only thirteen, Rex's grief inspired him to carry on his father's work in his own way. He began a collection of mounted birds, but with his natural instinct for line drawing, he began to conceive the idea of representing birds from life. When he studied the work of Audubon and other artists, he couldn't find the expressiveness he had seen in the eyes of living birds. So, he resolved to paint every bird in North America from life.

Rex realized he would need funds to travel the country to find many of the birds he wanted to paint. His first paid job, while still in his teens, was at Tiffany's, where he learned about color through an apprenticeship in copper-plate engraving. After learning the photoengraving business in Manhattan, he accepted a job in Portland, Maine, where he managed the photoengraving operation at a newspaper. Any spare time he had was spent in the backwoods sketching owls, hawks, and grouse. With his savings, he commissioned the construction of a sloop that he planned to sail down the Eastern Seaboard, sketching birds along the way. When the *Phalarope* was ready, Rex used whatever free time he had to explore the bays and inlets of the Maine coast, sketching shore birds.

In August 1895, Rex and his first mate set off from Portland Harbor, heading to Florida. They spent the better part of a year plying the coast, with stops in New Jersey, Delaware, Maryland, Virginia, the Carolinas, and Georgia, before ending the journey in the Florida Keys. During those months, Rex had numerous adventures and misadventures, but he ended the trip with hundreds of sketches of the native bird species he had encountered. After logging 2,740 miles on the waterways from Maine to Florida, in 1896 Rex sold the sloop, packed up his drawings and field notes, and returned by steamer to New York.

Back in Brooklyn, Rex began painting and playing the horses with his brother Charles. Using the $10,000 he won betting on a horse called Knight of the Garter, Rex funded a trip to the Midwest, the South, and along the Gulf Coast to observe and sketch more birds. Among his many adventures was an overnight stay at a moonshiner's cabin in the Great Smokies and meeting, at gunpoint, a former Confederate officer who invited him to dinner and showed him where to find the elusive ivory-billed woodpecker.

Rex tried to repeat his luck at the racetrack when he returned to New York. After losing $5,000 on an ill-advised bet on a horse, in 1899 Rex signed on to the *Eva and Annie*, a fishing boat out of Boston, as an opportunity to study ocean birds and earn money for his next trip. Spending weeks at a time at sea left Rex with a deep respect for his shipmates and for the power of the ocean. He also acquired a nautical vocabulary that he used liberally throughout the rest of his life.

With the money earned from fishing and some more lucky wagers, Rex traveled by train to Salt Lake City in the summer of 1901. Camping out at night, he spent his days on foot sketching birds he would never see back East—western jays, rosy finches, elf owls, and Inca doves among them. Outside Phoenix, he witnessed an epic battle in the desert between a roadrunner and a diamond-backed rattlesnake.

In Los Angeles, he took a job in a photoengraving shop for a few weeks and, after another fortuitous bet on a local horse race, boarded a train to San Francisco bound for Portland, Oregon. Rex traveled from the Willamette Valley, where he heard the varied thrush's evening call for the first time, through Montana to Idaho, making his way to Chicago, where he ended his last field trip. In 1904 he returned to Brooklyn to begin the process of painting, using the sketches and field notes he had sent home.

Rex had little regard for "the closet naturalist" whose "idea of a bird picture is whether bills or toe nails are the exact length." Although he briefly joined the Linnaean Society, he felt that many of its members had "a lack of vision and tolerance" and considered him "outside the sacred portals."

In 1907, Rex met Louis Agassiz Fuertes, the famous bird painter, who became a significant influence on his artistic methods as well as a good friend. Rex later described Fuertes as "the first American artist to portray birds life-like and accurately. None of his predecessors were artists and all their efforts caricatures. My contacts with him were all too few but study of his work helped wonderfully. . . . He was one of those rare souls, entirely without jealousy or smallness, willing and eager to share his immense store of knowledge. . . . He would look over my shoulder at a sketch. 'That's pretty good but how about rounding the head a little more, like this?' His swift, clever pencil traced the curve; it was always better than mine."

Rex destroyed all his own paintings twice, believing they were not good enough. He started over each time determined to paint better backgrounds as well as improved images of the birds. He wanted every detail of color to be correct, in particular the feet, eyes, and bill. Most of all he wanted his paintings to show "the beauty, courage and aliveness of feathered forms." But he also wanted his paintings to be accurate, so he began studying the vast collection of bird skins at the Museum of Natural History and perfecting his technique.

During the years Rex struggled financially while trying to complete his paintings, Katherine Marie Louise Brasher (known to family as Marie but to herself as Kay) supported Rex emotionally and financially. The daughter of Rex's half-brother, and seven years his junior, Kay was an educated and accomplished woman. After Rex's return from his last field trip out West, he and Kay lived in Brooklyn, Rex working on the paintings and Kay as a court reporter.

Around 1912 T. Gilbert Pearson, president of the National Audubon Society, paid Rex $750 to illustrate *Birds of North Carolina*, which allowed Rex and Kay to look for a place outside the city where Rex could paint without distractions. They purchased an abandoned farm on more than one hundred acres in Dutchess

County, New York, just across the state line from Kent, Connecticut. Rex named this narrow valley and the farm Chickadee Valley.

In 1913 Rex moved to the farm and spent most of his days renovating the old house inside and out, building a chicken coop, and amassing enough firewood to stay warm. He survived on pancakes, coffee, potatoes, and the occasional woodchuck stew. To produce income, he hired himself out as a carpenter so he could continue painting when time allowed. "Many pictures were completed under hard conditions. I would stoke all stoves, wrap my feet in a blanket and start." Meanwhile, Kay had become the confidential secretary to the young mayor of New York City, John Purroy Mitchel, so she delayed her move to join Rex, knowing her income was helping to continue his work.

Another commission in 1915, to illustrate key portions of *Nature Lover's Library*, edited by T. Gilbert Pearson and John Burroughs (who described Rex as "the greatest bird painter of all time"), gave Rex the freedom to keep painting. It also meant Kay could leave her job with the mayor and move to Chickadee Valley. Rex later recalled that those "days took on an atmosphere of content. We used the porch for a workroom. She typed by dictation, both finding in congenial work, surcease from old cares." Kay took over commissary and housework, permitting Rex more hours to paint. When funds were low, Rex sold his handcrafted weather vanes, door knockers, and birdhouses. Although money was always a worry, another commission from *Compton's Encyclopedia* and generous donations from several well-to-do friends kept Rex and Kay solvent.

Although Rex was content to live simply, he made certain improvements with Kay in mind, including laying a cedar floor in her bedroom and adding a large window in the kitchen. He notes in *Secrets of the Friendly Woods* that more than once he caught her "smiling rather pensively out of that aperture in a way she had not smiled before it was put there."

Kay's connections in the city brought writers, industrialists, and scholars to Chickadee Valley and generated interest in Rex. In 1925, through a meeting with Kay, Tom Wisehart produced a short article about Rex titled "Twentieth Century Audubon" that brought people from all over the country to Rex and Kay's door in Chickadee Valley. The subsequent publication of *Secrets of the Friendly Woods* brought even more attention to Rex, which encouraged him to reach a wider audience. At age fifty-five, instead of spending his days chopping wood and tending the garden, as he had imagined, he embarked on another seemingly impossible task.

Rex was determined to keep his collection of 874 paintings intact, but he also wanted them to be accessible to the public. He conceived a plan to reproduce the paintings as lithographs and produce five hundred sets of a twelve-volume edition. Rex, Kay, and Kay's brother, Phil Brasher, formed Rex Brasher Associates, and in May 1929 they began to solicit interest from potential patrons. Rex selected the Meriden Gravure Company in Connecticut to create the grayscale prints of the originals. The deal was sealed with a handshake.

When Rex announced his intention to publish *Birds and Trees of North America*, major industrialists and business leaders of the day such as William Keith Kellogg, William Boeing, and Richard Beatty Mellon ordered subscriptions for the set of books, which would be issued one volume at a time. Although the Great Depression led to multiple canceled subscriptions, Rex adapted by limiting the edition to one hundred. In four short years, with some young assistants, Rex completed the audacious project of hand-coloring the nearly ninety thousand prints required to publish the sets of books. With *Birds and Trees of America* "hailed as a masterpiece" by the *Baltimore Sun*, Rex was one of three artists included on *The Nation*'s honor roll for 1932, along with Thomas Hart Benton and Aaron Copland.

Rex was well aware that he never would have completed the paintings or published *Birds and Trees* without Kay. She ran their household, entertained their many visitors, and managed Rex's correspondence. Just as important, using her stenographic skills, Kay organized and typed the text that accompanies each plate, including scientific descriptions. Rex was also aware that Kay was seriously ill. Less than a year after the completion of *Birds and Trees*, in June 1933, Kay died at the age of fifty-five. Rex outlived her by decades, but her spirit never left him.

We cannot know the full nature of Rex and Kay's relationship. Throughout *Secrets of the Friendly Woods*, he refers to her as "the Commissary Department" and "the first mate." Rex's family members certainly regarded them as a married couple, though of course they could never have married given their blood relationship. We do know that they lived together for almost two decades, that they were devoted to each other, and that he grieved deeply for her. They were partners.

With the completion of *Birds and Trees* and the loss of Kay, Rex was intent on keeping his collection of paintings intact and preserved for the public. In 1934 he offered to donate the entire collection to the state of Connecticut on condition that the state construct a museum to display the paintings within two years. That fall, *Time* published a piece about the proposed museum, describing Rex as "more accurate than Audubon" given that he had spent most of his life "tramping across fields, swamps, beaches, spying on birds and recording their habits in warm colors that suggest Japanese prints."

Anticipating the completion of a museum, the *Hartford Courant* followed its progress, writing that "it would prove a mecca to all students of birds, from the beginner who knows only half a dozen species to authorities who would scrutinize minute details of Mr. Brasher's work. The plates give delight also to those who care more for trees and flowers than for birds, for these too Mr. Brasher has portrayed with faithfulness and spirit. Indeed his plates are so exquisite, so excellent in composition and in color, so much alive with knowledge and feeling for outdoor life, that many artists, particularly engravers and water colorists, find great pleasure in them without even noting the species of bird pictured."

Unfortunately, the state legislature was unable to authorize the needed funds for construction of the museum, and in January 1938 Rex retrieved the paintings from the basement of the Connecticut State Capitol and transported them to the headquarters of the National Geographic Society in Washington, DC. An exhibit of almost the entire collection, originally planned for one week, was extended for another week due to public interest. The

*Washington Evening Star* reported that seven thousand visitors viewed the paintings.

In 1940 the Connecticut legislature raised the money to purchase Rex's entire collection, with the intention of finding permanent exhibit space. Governor Robert A. Hurley commented that "the purchase, together with provision of a suitable home for the collection, would bring to a proper close a half century of such work as few naturalist-artists have ever done. Reproductions of the paintings are available in twelve-volume sets which, however, cost $2,500 apiece; Brasher wanted them made available to poor children and earnest teachers and amateur naturalists. The Connecticut purchase would do just that, so he feels that the job he set out to do is nearing the end."

Once again, timing was not on Rex's side. Soon after he delivered the collection to the state, World War II intervened, and the paintings were placed in protective storage in Hartford along with other priceless state records. In

1953 Rex's dream of having the paintings available to the public seemed to have been fulfilled when the collection was moved to the Harkness Estate in Waterford, Connecticut, where as many as sixty thousand people visited annually. Several years after Rex's death, curators began to fear that the watercolors were suffering from the humidity at the Harkness. The entire collection was relocated to the University of Connecticut's main campus in Storrs, where it remains today, well cared for but not exhibited to the public since 1988.

Similarly, the exquisitely crafted sets of *Birds and Trees of North America* are now either in private collections or housed at universities and museums, where they are in special collections and never seen by the public. In 1961 Rowman & Littlefield published a four-volume edition of *Birds and Trees* with revised and annotated text. Columbia University Press published a two-volume edition in 1968 containing fewer of the original illustrations. Unfortunately, the color reproduction of those editions did not capture the exceptional quality of the hand-colored plates in Rex's original volumes, and in any case, those later editions are now out of print and only occasionally available from rare-book dealers. Almost one hundred years after Rex Brasher completed his mission to represent every North American bird as a living creature, he has faded into obscurity.

Carl Rettenmeyer, the longtime director of the Connecticut State Museum of Natural History, explained the conundrum this way: Rex "sold very little work in his lifetime and this has been both an advantage and disadvantage. The advantage is that we have his work altogether in one place. The disadvantage is that he isn't as well known as he should be because his work did not go into museums and other collections."

Determined to change that, a small group of individuals formed the Rex Brasher Association in 2008, with the backing of Rex's two great-nieces, Deborah and Melode Brasher. Most of the founding members had personal connections to Rex and Chickadee Valley.

Despite his quest for uninterrupted solitude during the years he was painting, Rex was hardly a hermit. Visitors came to Chickadee Valley regularly, from near and far. Rex certainly counted men of means among his friends, some of whose generosity allowed him to complete his life's work. But he reserved his greatest respect for those who worked with their hands, such as the local men who knew how to wield an ax, manage a team of horses, or build a barn. My own grandparents and the grandparents of board members Janet Meade Reagon and Robert Meade were among those Rex counted as friends.

With this new edition of *Secrets of the Friendly Woods*, we hope that Rex Brasher will once again be recognized not only as a painter of birds but also as a man who devoted his life to leaving a record of North American birds in his time. As bird populations face increasing threats, we can learn a great deal from Rex's understanding and knowledge of bird behavior even as we admire the beauty of his art. Rex not only painted birds; he also *knew* them. His ability to capture birds in the fullness of life with his paintbrush and his words was extraordinary.

A century after the original publication of *Secrets of the Friendly Woods*, the Rex Brasher Association completed digitizing the twelve-volume edition of *Birds and Trees of North America*, thanks in large part to board members Munawar Ahmed and Matthew Schnepf. By making it available on our website, rexbrasher.org, we are honoring Rex's wish to share his work with the world. The University of Connecticut hopes to one day have a new space for regular exhibits of Rex's work. And thanks to the foresight and generosity of Deborah and Melode Brasher, Rex's great-nieces, the RBA will be able to preserve Rex's legacy on his beloved property in the friendly woods of Chickadee Valley. We are grateful to Jed Lyons and the Globe Pequot Publishing Group for believing in the enduring importance of Rex Brasher and reintroducing this exceptional man to a new audience. He has much to tell us.

Cynthia Carter Ayres
President, Rex Brasher Association

# SECRETS OF THE FRIENDLY WOODS

# SECRETS OF THE FRIENDLY WOODS

## CHICKADEE VALLEY

"WE 'LL give you one hundred and twenty-five dollars cash or ten cents apiece for every tie, cutting nothing under eight inches."

Nowadays this offer would seem of little moment, but when made, twelve years ago, it was something to be seriously considered. Hereabout, interchange of labor replaced cash to a large extent. To accept an offer of real money seemed advisable; it meant many months' freedom for artistic inclinations. Ten cents per tie undoubtedly would bring the total higher, but in scattered and deferred amounts. Although it was a long way ahead, I visualized the winter—slim pickin's without cash but a filled pantry with it! Just then one hundred and twenty-five dollars was really a great deal of money.

Intermittently the teams hauled load after load down the mountainside. Twenty-eight hundred ties and many thousand feet of lumber. Apparently I had lost one hundred and fifty-five dollars by accepting the cash offer.

One day in October Ed drove into our road behind a splendid pair of work-horses, to carry a load of our apples Dover way for cider. Ruddy-cheeked, clear-eyed (he 's the best shot and fisherman for miles around), straight forward, square—Ed is a fine type of the old New England pioneers.

"You 've had the rough end of the stick in this tie deal, Rex. Charlie and I have talked it over and we 're goin' to give you that hundred cords of slabs on the hill."

"Well, that 's certainly white of you, Ed! Guess I can use 'em."

In truth, they proved a real godsend. A chute was built, six hundred feet long, to the woodshed, thereby eliciting the remark from the road commissioner that I was the laziest man in Kent, for I shot my wood right into the kitchen.

Maybe . . . but that stack of cut wood saved many an hour with the ax and allowed me to swing a paint-brush instead. For over four years the slabs kept the stove going. Of course I mixed them with heavier stuff. "Rough end of the stick," eh? Why, they were worth one thousand dollars to me! It was real fun to put them in at the head and see them go skittering down against the butt. When the slide was wet, they *traveled*—make no mistake about that! After two or three of the heavier ones had threatened to demolish the north end of the house, I had to reduce their weight and speed by chopping them in two.

Those who attempted to dissuade me from burying myself alive, little understood either me or the possibilities. Another illustration of the individual's inclination to judge only from his own standpoint. For them the city held all that was desirable, and outside of it there could be nothing worth while. Mine was a different point of view and no regrets have come to me for following the solitary trail.

Seasons, birds, trees, sunrise . . . and *friends.* Wassaic way, Morris: alert, loyal, ready to help or give; a worker "from the heart out." Kent way, Ed: steady, dependable, kind, with the same readiness to lend a hand. And others. Fortunate indeed to count these men friends, for the type is fast vanishing. The finger of Fate which directed me here was this ad:

**FARM. One hundred fifty acres, half wood, half brook pasture, good house, barn and buildings. Terms reasonable.**

That was the lure,—cold type in the list of abandoned farms in New York State,—and I took it as a bluefish takes a squid. The usual line "near school and town" did not appear, and the omission added to its attractiveness. For years I had been roaming the woods, fields, and streams, gathering material for paintings of our North American birds, and I was looking for some remote spot where I could put into finished form the collection of sketches and notes. Behind lay the days when from the little *Phalarope's* deck I had watched suns rise and set. I lived for over a year on the sloop, traveling the intricate waterways down the eastern shore from Maine to Florida. Into the past, too, had gone the days afield which sometimes provoked the query: "Are you going to waste *all* your life? Are n't you ever going to settle down to *anything?*" et cetera.

Heredity came to my support: a descendant of seamen,—possibly of pirates!—should n't be affected by words. These ancestors had been accustomed to giving commands and would have received criticisms on the points of their swords. Alas, the days of the cutlass are gone! All one can do now is to take these gratuitous remarks as part of the job and forget them.

> Live as your manhood bids you live!
> From none save self expect applause.

A dreamer? Yes.

Everything man produces is formed first in his mind. We had no complete work, in color, of our birds, and my special dream was to produce one; for I loved those bits of feathered life and envied their control of a medium closed to man—the air. Objection? Yes, I know . . . aviation! But that is n't the way a bird flies. Man will never attain such proficiency unless he grows feathers and increases his muscular power about fifty times.

On the map, Dover Plains, New York, looked as close to the farm as Kent, Connecticut; so, early one March morning, two of us started from the former town. The winter had been open, the ground was bare, the air crisp and sharp. Redwings were *o-ka-leeing* along the banks of Ten Mile River. Little flocks of juncos flashed their white tail signals at frequent intervals and meadow-larks expressed a firm conviction that spring was here. We made for a little farm-house lying under the Taconic Hills ahead.

"How does the Ritton place, in the other valley, bear from here?"

"Right over there!" pointing east. "But I 'm telling you you 'd better take the road: it 's three miles across those mountains, and if you get into Wolf Swamp it 'll be a job getting out."

Around by Peaked Mountain we went nine miles, and the rough country we ran into returning across the range that afternoon showed us that taking that friendly caution had been wisdom.

The muddy road held back our eager feet, but the little white house under the lee of Buffalo Mountain came into view about ten o'clock. A veteran of the Civil War was caretaker. This fact prevented my expression of amazement when I discovered that every corner of the rooms had been utilized as tobacco-juice repositories! I am no believer in the rule, "Speak only good of the dead," but in this instance my restraint is a tribute to his soldierly qualities.

Examination showed the outside condition of the dwelling to be but slightly weathered: the most optimistic real-estate operator would not have had the assurance to insert the "near school and town" remark, in light of the farm's location—four miles from Kent and a quarter-mile off the main road; buried as far as it could be on the eastern slope of these Taconic Hills without ascending the mountain, but snuggled comfortably under old Buffalo. Winter nor'-westers would not strike us. It was a cheerful thought, for I was tired of wind. "My eyes grown dim from watching the sunwash on the brine" would recover among these friendly hills.

The house was built on a side slope, but a wall of large rocks (mainly dragged out of the ten-foot cellar excavation) had been erected just east of it, giving a level space all around where tin cans, old shoes, and other debris had been scattered with a liberal and careless hand. A two-foot-wide foundation sunk to the solid ledge meant permanency; even the worst sou'-

easter has failed to extract a tremor. The paint was still a protection, although beginning to peel. The price was small. We took the place.

There was much to do, but slight vision was necessary to see an attractive home a few years ahead.

The former owner, old Alonzo Ritton, was not only a moonshiner but a character. His specialty was metheglin, a derivative of fermented honey. I have never tasted it, but those familiar with this particular brand of lightning say it was real old forty-rod stuff. His principal business was its manufacture and distribution among the charcoal-burners who in his day were numerous among these hills. They say he collected most of their monthly pay. There must be some truth in this report, because he left five thousand dollars in the bank. It is certain he never accumulated that amount by working this collection of rocks as a farm.

Slowly the pencil marked off numbers on the

A. O. U. check-list, indicating a completed water-color. Storm outside meant more accomplished inside and winter always produced the largest number of marks. When the phœbe returned in March, perched on the porch roof, remarking emphatically, "Here-*be!*" and the song-sparrow's merry tinkle came from the willows, brush strokes grew more languid and some days the sable point was exchanged for a four-inch flat, and part of the house was painted. Oh, there was plenty to do! Outside, no guardian angel stood by to smooth out the creases: that had to be done with a hammer and saw. But inside—well, I don't think it wise to give too much praise: I might not get any dinner!

There was work, too, down the road; maybe a barn or a house to build. When the Commissary Department remarked that the supply of milk, coffee, and general provender was getting low, tools were gathered in a box and carried where there was financial use for them. When I was alone the problem of living bothered me little: one winter a flock of sixty Leghorns paid all expenses. My reputation for truth would evaporate if I were to tell here the weekly outlay. Within seventy-five miles of New York City, no telephone, no electric light, no car—and, what 's more, I don't miss them. (Sphinx-ian glances from party opposite.) Fill up the oil-barrel, the pantry, the cellar, and the wood-shed every autumn; shut the doors, keep stoves a-going . . . and paint!

Some years old Boreas *kept* the door shut. One winter six weeks went by before the snow road was broken out.

"How do you get to town?"

"Well, we own skis and snow-shoes. That 's one way; but mostly we don't."

Even a rough winter like that has its compensations: a lot more little marks made on the check-list. There were twelve hundred and one species and sub-species to do, plumage phases running this up into three thousand different figures, and over eighty per cent. of them life-size!

Years drifted by; the call of the sea grew faint, but here in this remote nook other notes awoke. The first robin against February snows. Atoms of crimson in bare apple boughs when the Ides of March bring a drift of purple finches. April: whitethroats with their notes of "crystal rain," peepers, and the woodcock's *scaip* when some mysterious impulse draws me to the window for a last look at every night which falls. May, with its chaos of exultant song. Even in July the wood-thrush's liquid notes at dawn and twilight. A wood-thrush and my favorite song-sparrow are having a duet now. A pair of black ducks which have nested in our meadow, winnowing past when they take their evening exercise flight. A grouse throbbing through the soft October haze. Foxes barking, and, rarer, weird screams of wildcats. Horned owls hooting under winter stars.

No, I do not miss the sea!

"Romance is dead," is the wail of the present. True, there are no more frontiers to conquer, Indians to pursue, or "letters of marque" authorizing us to scour the Seven Seas. Pirates? They, too, have disappeared save where in the far Formosan mists they glide upon the unwary trader. *Is* romance dead? Look around you! Artists at work on the casting for a new turbine . . . turning down a fifty-ton shaft at an enormous lathe . . . fitting delicate watch gears at a table . . . holding the throttle on a flyer . . . directing from the bridge the course of a liner. Adventurers all. Romance gone? *No!* Only following different trails.

Perhaps the greatest adventure is to know what you want to do, and do it. If this is true, mine was finished when all the little feathered fellows were portrayed on paper and snugly stowed away in a fireproof studio.

There 's another adventure ahead: the sunset gun. If any sounds of earth do travel into the Infinite, I hope to hear the veery singing from the hemlocks in early dawn or when that weird pale-green light fills the valley after a squall has passed.

## WHO'S WHO IN THE BLUE

### I

WHEN the government dredge finished gnawing its way down the Indian River it was decided to cut through the narrow ribbon of beach and tow the big thing north on the broad Atlantic. Unless scouring tide conditions are right, artificial inlets along the eastern coast seldom remain open. Frequently the first norther will close them completely, smoothing over the sand until none would guess an opening had ever been made.

All day under double reefs the sloop *Phalarope* had logged a steady seven knots down the Indian River, reaching Gilbert's Cut at four bells in the late afternoon. Sheets were flattened. With wind abeam the sloop flew, the crescendo of surf deepening to a steady roar. The mighty Gulf Stream, driving on a good five miles an hour into the teeth of half a gale, was heaving shoreward tremendous waves which burst upon the outer reef scarcely one hundred yards from the beach. Here the hundred-fathom curve came close to shore and the twelve-foot seas were crashing upon the barrier unchecked by shoal water.

Tacking back and forth on the sheltered mill-pond inside, two men on the sloop watched the display of limitless power.

"Old Nep is certainly paddling his fingers around something outrageous! I guess we won't stick our bowsprit into those fellows to-night—get a ducking sure," remarked the skipper.

"That goes as you said it. Fine chance we 'd have of making Lake Worth Inlet in this smother! The lee of Sewell's Point will look good to me," said the mate.

Toward that point we drove. The mainsail swung inboard as land blanketed the wind. A figure before a fire on the shore hailed us.

"Sloop ahoy!"

"Ahoy yourself!"

"You boys come ashore and have supper with me?"

"All right!"

Have you ever eaten fresh fried pompano in the open, with the trade-winds snoring through palmettos overhead? If not, do it! Your life is n't complete until that experience has been yours.

"Maine? You come from there? Why, Harpswell 's my home town! Shake again! Came down here three years ago on a Portland schooner and been driftin' around ever since. Stay two winters and you 're gone. Blood thins out so you can't stand a New England winter. Just now I 'm running a string of gill-nets. Been doing pretty well, too, until I sprained my wrist two days back."

"We 'll string your gear for you until your hand gets better."

"Well, I guess you fellows know how to do it. Seems like an answer to prayer, though

I never made any. You boys must be Christians."

"No; Blue Domers and Golden Rulers!"

"Never heard of 'em! Anyway, you 're *white.*"

Literally, this statement was scarcely true: we were tanned a warm shade of umber brown; but metaphorically . . .

Next morning we boated the two gill-nets, the owner going along to show us where to make the best sets. These nets are only four feet deep, and for two men who had handled heavy purse-seines on a Gloucesterman it was child's play getting this light twine overboard. When it was all wet we shipped our oars, lighted pipes, and lay by for an hour before underrunning.

A fish-hawk came into view, flying down the St. Lucie River. About an eighth of a mile away he paused, fluttering, in the air.

"Watch that fellow; he 's going to strike!"

Strike he did, like a six-pound heaving-lead. As he dropped, a bald eagle shot from his lookout perch ashore and dived downward. The white-headed robber had waited until the osprey was falling on his prey. But something was wrong! Instead of rising with a fish in his rough blue-gray claws, the osprey was thrashing violently and being dragged through the water. With the menacing freebooter above, the unmanageable fish below, our friend had fallen into trouble.

"He 's hooked something that 's too big to lift and can't let go. Out oars! We 've got to rescue him before he 's dragged under."

By the time we reached the scene of conflict the hawk was nearly drowned. He had been hauled repeatedly beneath the surface and each time a longer interval elapsed before his reappearance.

"A grouper, and a fifteen-pounder at that!" exclaimed the skipper, unhooking the hawk's talons from the fish's back. "What in thunder did you think you were doing, tacklin' a fish like that?—Lucky it was n't heavier or you 'd have been a goner."

The osprey was thrashing violently and being dragged through the water

Even had the bird been capable of answering, he was too exhausted to do so, lying in the bottom of the boat, gasping for air. Rowing ashore, we placed him on the warm beach and watched him slowly recover, to wing his way languidly off.

The whole proceeding doubtless puzzled the eagle, but it did not scare him away from the locality. That same afternoon we saw him swoop down over another fish-hawk (it may have been the rescued one), frighten it into dropping its catch, then, in a lightning continuation of the same sweep, seize the relinquished prey before it struck the water. The old villain had speed enough for that feat, yet was too lazy to do his own fishing. Maybe he did n't like a bath!

II

Now while we have the country's emblem upon the screen, let us shift the scene—an easy task for the writer and scarcely less difficult for the reader. The back drop is a small mountain rising sheer, on its south and east sides, six hundred feet; on the west the ascent is more gradual, and from the north it is possible to drive a horse to the summit. The side scenes are hills, but with more rolling contours. Between lies Chickadee Valley, on the eastern edge of Dutchess County, close to the Connecticut line.

Fifteen years ago Peaked Mountain was covered with splendid pines, and on one of the ledges a pair of eagles had their home. Those trees and birds have disappeared, the former under the lumberman's saw and the latter probably by the gun of some cheap murderer. Although wofully scarce in this section, eagles are not entirely extinct. Every year I see one or more of their soaring forms against the blue, the sunlight glistening on snow-white head and tail. Their keen eyes no longer monopolize the wonderful tapestry of field, forest, and river spread far beneath. Man's longing to soar in this illimitable air and view earth's panorama from unstable heights has materialized. True, he does not do it with the eagle's ease, grace, and silence, but 't is accomplished. Perhaps, when mastery of the air becomes more nearly perfect, man's thoughts and mind will broaden like the wide spaces below the aviator's vision.

Three years ago, while picking huckleberries atop Buffalo Mountain, a mile northwest of the house, I saw an eagle coasting through the intervale below, and for the first time I looked upon the back of this majestic bird in flight. How easily he slipped along—pinions motionless, wide-stretched, the perfection of effortless progress!

Last summer the roof needed re-shingling and one day I was hard at the task. A shadow swept across. Overhead, within fifty feet, a fine, pure dusky-black, immature bald-head glided along. A quarter of a mile away, like a bolt of black lightning, he shot earthward. I rushed below for the glasses and just caught a glimpse of something twisting in his claws before the windbreak of hemlocks intervened. It was probably a woodchuck, although the distance was too great for me to be certain.

Next day, while I was finishing the ridge, the "noblest Roman of them all" appeared. With quick, impetuous wing-beats a duck-hawk (one of the few true falcons) flew leisurely by, reconnoitering. Watching, I hoped some quarry would wake him to action, for there is always a thrill in the sight of this imperial bird at top speed. Some automobile manufacturers boast their cars will accelerate from five to fifty miles in eight seconds. Slow! Here is a machine which can shift from fifteen to sixty in one second! To tempt him into a "stoop," I should almost have been willing to have him mistake my head for a rabbit! There 's nothing in telepathy, for he went on over the hill with that characteristic flight which enables an observer to identify him when he is merely a black speck in the distance.

Several years ago a pair of duck-hawks preempted a home site in the Palisades opposite New York City, making frequent visits to town after the pigeons which constituted a large proportion of their food—a rather interesting instance of the extremity to which adaptation to enviroment can be carried. Here was a pair of these impetuous birds, normally at home in the wildest fastnesses, doing their hunting in city streets and on housetops. I have seen them perched on the Brooklyn Bridge towers, where they seemed strangely out of place, the ultimate contrast between primitive nature and the apex of civilization.

Of course every bird "bug" considered a visit to the nest a sacred duty, and toward that spot they gravitated like Mohammedans to Mecca, with the result that those unfortunate falcons had even less privacy than Irving Cobb's famous goldfish.

But they were game, and notwithstanding innumerable peering heads probably would have raised a family, had not some "enterprising collector" sneaked down at night and stolen the eggs. I have no doubt a large percentage of the audience coveted those treasures, but the majority would have voted a firing-squad for the actual thief—may his shadow grow thin!

The peregrines' unhesitating courage and readiness to attack occasionally lead them into surprising situations. One November day, concealed among the reeds in a blind, I was contemplatively smoking and seriously considering broaching the luncheon puncheon, when a projectile shot over and hit one of the decoys, knocking its head completely off. The only one of the three participants of this incident exhibiting no astonishment was the wooden imitation. The falcon was more than nonplussed: he flew off as though actually chagrined, perhaps because his aim was poor in hitting the head instead of the back. That was the only time I have ever seen this fierce and domineering bird exhibit indications of feeling like a fool. Many thanks, fair Fate, for directing his attack to the fraudulent duck instead of the jug!

In describing the falcon's onslaught some

writers state it rakes the body of its victim with its claws. This may add extra "gory dramatic" to the recital, but as actual natural history it is open to question. In every instance which I have observed, when a duck-hawk strikes, its claws are driven in and remain there. Usually victim and aggressor come to earth together, or the hawk releases his grip just before reaching the ground. Even over water I have seen the pursuer hang on with the spray flying about him until the quarry's struggles lessened and the hawk carried it off. It is true duck-hawks will harry flocks of small birds,—sandpipers, blackbirds, et cetera:—seize one after the other, and squeeze and drop them; but no large victim I have examined showed any raking slashes; simply round wounds where the hawk's sharp nails had entered.

Part of the duck-hawk's Latin name, *peregrinus* (meaning "wandering"), is somewhat of a misnomer, although the genus, with slight geographical difference in coloration, is cosmopolitan. Our native birds have a strong predilection for certain areas, returning year after year to the same locality. In winter they follow migrating shore birds some distance south, doubtless finding open hunting easiest. In one day I have counted eight winging south along the beach before an October nor'wester.

Courage is largely a matter of physical condition: if the heart is strong and functioning properly, you have it. Man's primitive instincts still are sufficiently in the ascendant to make us admire bravery even in a pirate, while utterly contemptuous toward cowardice. Frequently our attitude toward the latter should be one of pity. With that strange inconsistent reasoning still applied by many when considering certain ethics, even a coward despises a coward. The duck-hawk epitomizes courage, speed, fearlessness. Although we know he is a freebooter, running down and capturing birds as large as—yes, larger than—himself (even the swift carrier-pigeons falling before his

A projectile shot over and hit one of the decoys, knocking its head completely off

whirling onslaught); although we find remains of many friendly and beneficent species scattered around his aery, do we drag out a gun and drop him among his victims? We do not. We regret that he is such a ruthless killer, and let it go at that. His dashing prowess saves him from that fate, and yet his species is decreasing. Each year the number lessens: last year I saw not one duck-hawk.

To alter an erroneous belief which has been forming for generations is a long and difficult undertaking. Most farmers of this locality are sure the red-tailed hawk is a hen-hawk. I have tried to eradicate this notion, but with only partial success. Rarely an individual develops a fondness for poultry; then, of course, it becomes necessary to destroy him, but the majority of redtails live on humble game and eliminate many destructive forms of life.

During mild winters a few hardy ones remain and to-day (the thirteenth of December) although snow squalls and sunshine follow one another in extended areas of shadow and light across the valley, I hear the wild, shrill call of the redtail.

Most birds of prey can exist for a considerable period of time without food, but this hawk's indifference to hunger is phenomenal. One day last winter a pair of redtails were attempting to catch a grouse; working together they may accomplish this, although I have never seen it done. The quarry took refuge in brush under a steep cliff and one of the pursuing hawks lit atop a hickory six hundred feet from the house of a friend of mine. At the crack of my friend's rifle the bird fell, recovered, and flew off, both legs dangling. Six weeks afterward that unfortunate bird was found half a mile away, near the road, and still alive. The hunger, cold, and pain it must have endured were too ghastly to think about. Even as I write this there is a weak feeling in my amidships' section at the mere recollection.

Victims wounded by my own gun caused me to shelve it thirty years ago. The incident just related is not a cheerful one, but I speak of it for two reasons: first, in the hope it may keep some one from destroying the next harmless hawk; secondly, to prove what unbelievable courage and fortitude this form of life possesses.

On a clear May morning I watched one of a pair (probably the male) who build their home every year in a near-by hemlock, start those wonderful sweeping circles. Up, up he went out of unaided eyesight, but still plainly visible through the glasses. For an hour and ten minutes he wove those aërial spirals without moving a wing!

III

When emerald nubbins of wild cabbage push their way through brown April soil, a lithe ash-colored bird glides deliberately over ochre hillocks of bog-grass, quartering the ground as carefully as a well-trained hunting-dog.

Years ago this meadow yielded a fair amount of hay, but each season the water backed up farther and farther until the ground became too soft for horses. If reclaimed land is not cut over regularly, the jungle soon seizes it. To-day, alders, white birches, elms, and maples are rapidly changing it to a tangled miniature forest. Every spring one, sometimes two, pairs of marsh-hawks successfully add to the harrier population, conditions for such consummation being particularly favorable. One small cleared spot near the center of the field is sufficiently elevated to be above water under normal conditions, but surrounded with marshy ground wet enough to prevent raids by foxes or coons. It is selected yearly for one of the nests.

Two or three days after the male's advent an umber-brown female appears and goes directly to the site of last year's nest, the male hovering a few feet above while she inspects the premises. Sometimes she decides at once; other years they both wander up and down the valley for a week, apparently uncertain where to settle. This is only stratagem, however, for they invariably return to the familiar site, and both pitch into the home-building task wholeheartedly.

A good foundation of small dead limbs and twigs is first put down and then the living-quarters of the nest woven of coarse weathered grasses and reeds—a remarkably well-put-together structure for a hawk, most of this genus being rather careless home-builders.

Notwithstanding a generous wing area, the marsh-hawks are rather slow fliers, lacking entirely the dash and speed of a Cooper or a sharp-shinned hawk. There are times, though, when the male—swinging in great semicircles—pauses at the top of his sweep, drops with a falcon's speed, turns tail overhead, drops again, somersaults, and rises straight up under the push of the north wind, to repeat the ambitious ecstasy perhaps a dozen successive times.

I stood on the little June Bridge one keen April morning, with half a gale hurtling down the valley, watching this dizzy courting. Absolutely oblivious of my presence, the performer swept by within a few feet of me, repeatedly;

his mate on a near-by fence rail was equally indifferent. She seemed to be aware of nothing in the world except her dashing lover. Some sweeps were made in silence save for a swishing sound of wings: others terminated with a raucous *ca-ca-ca-ca-ca-er.*

"If you 'd put that speed into hunting, old boy, nothing a-wing could get away from you. I 'm glad you don't, though!—mice and snakes or even 'snips and snails and puppy-dogs' tails' will make our friendship wax and grow."

I suppose the marsh-hawks caught *some* birds, but I never detected our valley hawks in the act. Redwings, kingbirds, and swallows regularly took their "daily dozen" in bluff attacks, but the harriers soon became accustomed to the bombardment and paid no heed whatever to these attentions.

When the young were hatched, in early June, food in the vicinity had been well thinned out. While one parent remained near the nest the other went on more extended scouting expeditions. A favorite hunting-ground was on a hill a mile south, where an artificial trout-pond supplied a bountiful spread of frogs. The guardian parent would see its returning mate long before I could, and with loud cries of welcome, rise to meet the successful hunter. In July, when the youngsters had learned to use their wings, they were quick to imitate this manœuver: with five hungry squealing feathered babies circling wildly around there was pandemonium in the valley. Regular Newspaper *Row*, when newsboys fought for their papers.

When close enough to make identification possible through the glasses, one found that mice, moles, snakes, or frogs were the provender distributed—no birds.

In early September the entire family gathered in circling conclave and discoursed with loud and insistent earnestness upon some important subject, probably their winter home, and then suddenly disappeared.

I hope it will be an early spring. Mr. Circus's courtship makes an interesting and exciting moving-picture.

## BR'ER GROUSE

THE sun pencil through the western oriel window moves slowly up the wall and at half-past three o'clock winks out. The shadow of Buffalo Mountain reaches across the valley, climbs the white birches, ascends East Mountain, transforming its snow-clad sides to dusky mauve. The narrowing ribbon of light above glows deep orange, tips the highest summits, and disappears.

Expectantly we wait at the north window. Almost on the stroke of five, hurtling forms emerge from the hemlock windbreak, shoot straight toward the house, swerve, and alight among the orchard trees for their supper of apple-buds.

It is seldom a living form epitomizes so admirably its environment: capable, strong, and hardy as the stern hills where it lives, this king of game-birds will survive long after its

Repeatedly, the performer swept by within a few feet of me

more susceptible brothers have vanished. Only one combination of the elements is fatal: when deep snows become ice-covered while birds are beneath, the feathered creatures perish. Fortunately this catastrophe does not happen frequently. The man with a gun is not their worst enemy. Probably more grouse take the Long Trail in the first three weeks of their existence than in the entire following period.

The art of repose has disappeared from modern life. The hope of recapturing some of it lured us to this spot in the Taconic Hills, and the quest has proved successful. Humanity, chattering like Otter Brook in spring flood, has dwindled to a minor note. Yes, of course there are times when the noise is renewed, but the road is rough! Only hardy spirits push their cars over it; and, oddly enough, most of these adventurers are congenial fellows who do not demand an incessantly audible vocabulary as a mark of friendship. Instead of tom-cats stalking across back-yard fences, I see a mother grouse lead a flock of youngsters over the road not forty feet away: instead of yowls from the aforesaid felines, I catch, perhaps, the stamp of a deer startled from the orchard when I open the windows at night.

Late March, and the age-old battle between snow and sun is on again: hillsides change from white to gray as the southern sides of rock emerge. Patches of brown appear—last autumn's carpet of leaves, which has not yet melted into the soil. The boisterous month wanes, snowy areas lessen, and at midday the thin steamy snow-fog wraiths gather in depressions. Wavering April comes hesitatingly down the valley, and indefinite spots of white saxifrage, like ghosts of tiny snow-drifts, dot the open hill spaces. Then through the still, warm air comes a sound as of distant blasting: the first booms have a distinct interval between them, but gradually the tempo increases to continuous notes which merge into a subdued roar. Br'er Grouse is sending a challenge and invitation abroad from the old hemlock log a few hundred feet west of the house.

By synchronizing each advance with the drumming—for apparently the bird is deaf and blind during the performance—one may approach without much difficulty, and the stalking is well worth the effort. Careful, now! He is just beyond that bunch of witch-hazel. There he goes again—and we cover the last ten yards to the red-oak within forty feet of him.

When you hear the first note of resumption, peek around the trunk. There he is, erect as a mitered bishop, tail wide-spread and flattened on the log for support, ruffs half opened, wings moving with increasing rapidity until at the apex they are merely a blur.

Winter is slipping fast astern. Love is awakening, and this "soft half Syrian day" hints that real spring is not far away on the weather bow. The drumming is repeated. Twenty feet away, beneath a half-opened frond of ferns, a female walks with hesitating steps; apparently indifferent—like all her sex—she comes into the open, stopping frequently to pick up an imaginary titbit or to throw a dead leaf carelessly over her back. But indifference is a game which two can play, for King David on the log pays no attention to her advent until she is within five feet of his throne. He drums again, and in the middle of the rolling notes she jumps upon the log. Does he stop? He does *not!* The penetrating muted tumult continues to the end, while the lady preens a wing . . . stops while running a primary through her bill . . . and looks at him in surprise.

"My goodness! Where did you come from? This is my boudoir, really. Rather an intrusion on your part!"

They are all touched with the same wand—of dissimulation—bird, animal, or human.

Now comes a change in the performance, given few of us to witness, and only when Fate is unusually kind. His tail is raised from the log, extended to its fullest; his ruff spread almost in a circle, giving the illusion of a disembodied head. With tail and ruff nearly meeting, wings extended stiffly downward, he

A mother grouse led a flock of youngsters over the road

turns slowly around, like a manikin on a pedestal. The exhibition of pomp, beauty, and pride, generously shown from all angles, is too much! The overawed and subdued lady succumbs.

This imitation of a miniature turkey does not always follow the drumming: in fact, I have noted it but twice.

The feathered little Don Juan sometimes is so puffed up with pride and excitement that he will strut his stuff before an unconcealed onlooker. Those fortunate enough to meet one so generously inclined will never forget the picture of pomposity and self-complacency paraded before his eyes.

Among masters of word-painting, Lafcadio Hearn ranked high. Although it is many years since I first read his "Memory of Last Island," the extraordinary beauty of his concise descriptions is still vivid. There is more or less of an imitative streak in all of us. We, unconsciously perhaps, follow the style which appeals most strongly. What goes down on paper may be far removed from the master hand, but here and there we form words into a sentence which betrays us. After all, we are but imitators of those who have traveled ahead, with just a tiny leavening of originality. Here was one who seemed worthy of following, and then along came those blank moving-picture captionists and knocked that soaring ambition into bits. No writer would dare start a paragraph to-day with the words: "Came the dawn"!

Well, that 's just what happened one day in early April; and with the dawn came a smoke-filled valley. Compared with the holocausts which sweep the Western and Northern mountains of our country, these fires are minor affairs because conifers are isolated, and only among pines, spruces, and hemlocks do we get the terrible "crown" fires. Hereabout the fires generally are ground blazes menacing only when they reach a mass of tie-mill slashings.

They do damage enough, however. If brush or leaves have accumulated at the foot of a deciduous tree, flames will burn the bark deeply and kill the tree. Add destroyed grouse homes, scorched arbutus and other wild-flower beds, and the price grows.

At the foot of Preston Mountain the truck was waiting. Shovels, grub-hooks, and buckets were thrown aboard. Not the least strenuous part of that wild day was the business of hanging on to the four-cylindered steed as it leaped ponderously from crag to crag, like a certain goat! Sitting nonchalantly on the driver's seat was my old friend Jo Chase, smoking his pipe and guiding that bucking bronco with the aplomb of a city chauffeur steering a Packard on a cement boulevard. Numerous tufts of hair sticking through holes cut in the felt, held his hat on—a simple and convenient scheme obviating a chin strap!

"Ye gods!" exclaimed Bill, when an unusually stiff bump lifted us a foot.

"Ditto!" I remarked. "Save the buckets!"

The fire had been held to the south'ard of the Dover Road, and our job was to keep it from running north and east. The lay of the land was favorable. We back-fired along the edge of an open strip, and the draft from the main conflagration sucked our blaze inward. There was considerable green grass, and areas comparatively free from leaves, so killing the outer rim of the back-fire was not difficult. With a small wet cedar it was swiped out almost as fast as I could walk.

In this half-mile patrol I found one grouse nest with thirteen eggs. When the men came in, toward noon, they reported finding and saving three more. A plot of arbutus gave me a lively fifteen minutes, but finally was saved —only the edges scorched. By nightfall we had the flames under control, but not until nearly eight thousand acres had been burned over.

All this because one man refused to sell a

He turns slowly around like a manikin on a pedestal

wood-lot to another! There was no definite proof: if there had been, I think we should have hanged the criminal! But that was the consensus of opinion, and these men belong to a type which is seldom wrong. "Slowly, with many stumblings, man climbs upward." *Slowly* is right, else a thing masquerading in the guise of a man would not have destroyed so many wild lives because of spite toward a neighbor. A single burned grouse would have outweighed the paltry essence he might have called his soul—though in so defining it he would have been alone. Individuals of his grade would seem to possess no soul.

The feverish restlessness permeating the world to-day, would disappear if we could emulate the simplicity and straightforward lives of the woods people. In the long flight leading upward the step ahead is marked "Consideration." Some have their feet upon it, some have put it behind, but far too many are lagging. A backward glance shows such uncounted millions that the heart sinks, hope dims. Will they ever make the grade? Perhaps. We are learning. But a long interval of destruction may intervene.

Suddenly up through the forest gloaming
A partridge rose and that urgent whirring
Startled our breath and checked our roaming:
We stood and were still where the leaves were
stirring.

## THE TUFF TRIUMVIRATE

### I

THE receptacle where the least lovely kitchen tasks are performed stands against the north wall. Facing a blank space while cleaning up throws one's thoughts back where they don't belong, so a window eighteen by twenty-four was cut through the wall and a pane of clear glass permanently fastened there. It changed more than the room inside. The cookie, of course, is normally good-natured,—I should n't dare say anything else,—but I caught her more than once smiling rather pensively out of that aperture in a way she had not smiled before it was put there.

Within this frame are painted many pictures, each one a masterpiece. Sometimes they are changed often each day. The back drop varies least—an upright dark-green hemlock windbreak, the same through all seasons except in spring when the green lightens a little or darkens when a storm is foot-loose.

The hundred-foot space between, changes with each day ticked from the calendar. Snows of March displaced by fainter imitations of saxifrage and bolder splashes of shad-bush cream. Summer's infinite varieties of green, most difficult to catch with a brush, the exquisite shades of autumn, and elusive purple and browns of winter follow one another, exhibit their wonders, fade, and find heart anew.

Along in February, if the snow chances to be deep, about five o'clock in the afternoon (you can almost set your watch by them), we watch the ruffed grouse shoot out of the evergreens, sweep down with curved wings past the house, and alight in the apple-trees for their evening meal of buds. Individuals sometimes lose control or forget to use their steering-gear,

A goshawk hit the bird with extended talons

for twice they have kept on coming until they plumped smack into the clapboards. Fortunately, neither was seriously hurt. One was knocked unconscious: I held him in my hand for five minutes before he revived. Coming to, he looked around inquiringly as though asking, "Where am I?" There was no doubt at all that the location was not desirable, for he left it in a flash.

Some winters the first mate's longing for the white lights grows too intense to resist and I become a real honest-to-goodness hermit. On one of these occasions, while making a pretense of washing the dishes (I am informed that I never have learned how!) but really watching six grouse which were feeding on grain scattered just beyond the grape-arbor and within thirty feet of the window, I saw one of the birds straighten up and turn its head rapidly from side to side. Vision uphill was obstructed by part of the house, but my curiosity was soon satisfied. A goshawk hit the bird with extended talons, claws wide apart, both rolling in a flurry of feathers over and over downhill. The hawk's claws evidently had not struck through to the body; he was striving for a death-grip and trying to stun the grouse with blows of his bill.

Grabbing a gun, I rushed to the rescue. Happily the grouse's struggles had been sufficiently strenuous to hold off his antagonist and at my entrance into the fracas the hawk arose, flying directly toward me. Thinking he intended alighting on a post between, I withheld fire. Alas! he swung by within twenty feet! A splendid fully grown, dark slate-blue bird. The rifle cracked—if it had only been a shot-gun!—but that perfect aërial machine disappeared on wings which whistled as he went into high.

Meanwhile the near-victim had gathered himself together and hidden snugly in a rock-crevice under the hemlocks. The other five all crowded under protective briers or small bushes and it was fully ten minutes before their courage returned. During that interval they did not move even an eyelid. Frightened enough they were then, but life's hazards evidently are soon forgotten, for next day at the regular time all six were back eating supper, nonchalantly.

Though swift of wing, the goshawks lack the accuracy of aim and persistency in pursuit exhibited by the noble hawks. Singularly enough, the youngsters with their brown backs and stripes below seem to have more tenacity of purpose than the old ones. I saw one of these immature birds dive into a hawthorn bush after a rabbit. The branches were so thick that he could not reach the quarry, but he struck again and again, at each attack leaving a bunch of feathers hanging on the thorns. I walked toward the scene of action, but apparently the bird did not see me at all. Every sense seemed concentrated on the desire to kill. I was within ten feet of him before he desisted, swinging off denuded of half his apparel. Bunny never made a move, either being paralyzed by fear or knowing that leaving that shelter with its thickly clustered spiked branches meant death. Fright had benumbed it so completely that though I reached down and stroked its ears and back it did not move. Fear reacts among many forms of life in two directions—often as a protection, sometimes as a means of extinction. I have seen rabbits bolt like a brown streak for a hole and reach it. Others stop suddenly in the open and are easily captured by the pursuer. Nature is an impartial old dame, sometimes assisting the helpless, sometimes forgetting entirely and offering them up as a sacrifice to any rapacious pursuer which needs a meal.

It is fortunate for the ruffed grouse that goshawks are not numerous and that their winter visitations are infrequent. I have never seen more than five in a winter, and probably have seen the same bird more than once; and some cold seasons go by without a glimpse of one. If the snow is deep and soft, they catch very few grouse, for the pursued bird will dive into the white blanket and, once beneath its shelter, is safe; a hawk never attempts to go in after one.

I was sitting, one January day, on the bank of a small tributary of the Androscoggin River in Maine, with my back against a friendly birch, idly puffing the old pipe and enjoying the comparatively warm sunshine. It had been a regular winter,—steady cold and three feet of snow on the level,—but that day the January thaw was on and the temperature must have touched forty degrees. A whir of wings broke my meditation; a grouse shot past from behind, so close that the disturbed air fanned my cheek, and dove into the snow on the opposite bank. Mingling with the whir of its pinions came a thin whistling as a fine blue-gray form dashed in pursuit not ten feet behind. The interval was enough and the foiled pirate swung upward in a long curve, the sun glinting for an instant on his fierce ruby eye. No moving picture has ever thrilled me like the breathless action of that near-drama. It happened years ago, but even now as I record the scene a faint touch of the electric sensation reawakes.

## II

As I was trying with a piece of nut-meat, to entice a chickadee to my finger, standing at the end of a short walk above the ten-foot stone wall east of the house, the black-capped atom flew under my hand, alighting on the rail, and there crouched motionless. The next instant a slim pointed-winged bird swept directly toward me through the apple boughs and I met it with a side swipe of my hat. The blow did not knock it off its wing, but diverted its course to one side, and that chickadee's life was saved, at least for the moment. The enemy was a Cooper hawk, and a hungry one. What must have been a disconcerting incident—being slapped with a hat—did not scare it beyond the walnut-tree scarce fifty feet away.

A hurried entrance into the house, a grab

at the twenty-five caliber! The upright form was still there when I peered out at the back door; and then . . . it was n't! Forty years have not diminished the hope that each time afield I shall see something new, learn a novel habit of a bird or animal, and that expectation is seldom disappointed. As the years roll by, this anticipation makes me reluctant to destroy *any* life, because from a dead thing we learn nothing—save anatomically! But I must admit a sense of satisfaction when I drop one of these arch-villains.

Civilized mankind makes premeditation a necessary preliminary to first-degree murder, and insists all accused shall have a trial. But when an individual runs amuck, shooting every one in his path, we waive both the preliminary and the trial. Self-preservation demands that we destroy that particular brand of killer on the spot, and we proceed to do just that. Here before the bar we have a duplicate of the human maniac, a bird who loses all sense of restraint, and kills not for food but for the delight it finds in slaughter. A regular feathered mink, but infinitely more harmful to the avian world, because it has wings of such power and speed that few escape.

Among the numerous times I have seen the Cooper hawks strike I recall only three instances when the attacked bird escaped. An intervening limb saved a robin; a pair of catbirds separated as the hawk dove, thereby diverting his aim; a meadow-lark was driven into a grass tussock and by some miracle slipped out beneath his talons, which evidently had not penetrated. The Cooper hawk has the most impetuous and accurate aim of all the small hawks. The duck-hawk perhaps is his equal in accuracy, but I know of no other. Systematists have placed the Cooper among the ignoble hawks, as he lacks the extra tooth in the bill. That is all he does lack, though! In speed, courage, and fierceness he is the peer of many of the so-called noble birds.

One spring I raised, with a brooder, some Leghorn chicks. When they were about half-grown I heard them, one day, talking excitedly behind the chicken-house, and, turning the corner, I almost stepped on a Cooper hawk rapidly and efficiently tearing one of them into small pieces. There is only one thing more of a fool than a chicken—another one! There they stood, cheeping and peering at the anatomical exploitation of one of their number—and within a foot of the dissector! Perhaps their lack of a real, live mother deprived them of a proper terror of hawks. Young chicks not artificially reared certainly possess this fear—and all, whether reared naturally or incubatorially, refuse fox-meat, though eager for any other kind. One hereditary instinct is passed on, while the other seems withheld. Mr. Wiggam, Mr. Kellogg, and the Tennessee Legislature please note!

## III

In habits, impetuosity, blood-thirst, in color—in fact, in everything except size—the little sharp-shinned buccaneer is an exact replica of his relative the Cooper. The superior size of the latter enables him to accomplish more destruction, but ounce for ounce there is little difference between the two villains. The Cooper prefers to stage his onslaught upon domestic "game" in the open, depending upon celerity of attack to get away with the spoils before an onlooker can seize a weapon. Poultry farms without shrubbery suffer the most, and unceasing vigilance is necessary to prevent these twin bolts of blue-gray gathering in their daily quota of chicks.

Foxes and some hawks are shrewd enough to refrain from hunting in the vicinity of their homes. Not so with the sharp-shinned: a pair will exterminate song-birds for a considerable area around the nesting site, and if they take up their abode near by, you will have to get them or they will destroy a large percentage of your feathered neighbors. Find the nest, get within gunshot, and do the deed. I hesitated long and considered all sides of the question before advising the elimination of any life, but in the case of goshawks, Cooper hawks, and the sharp-shinned, the judgment is against them. Every observer, as far as I know, upholds this decision. These three hawks literally are pirates of the air—regular winged Morgans, Teaches, and Kidds among the defenseless wayfarers of the hills and valleys.

But even the villain of a drama may have moments when the demon within prods—or, rather, spurs—him into an act which results beneficially. Watching a small bunch of friendly chickadees feeding on the porch one April day, I saw them all suddenly "freeze." This capacity of theirs for recognizing an enemy is an interesting and remarkable faculty, and sudden cessation of motion always means "enemy in sight!" And there he was on the extreme tip of an apple-tree limb, a dark-gray shrike. Now, as a rule I let this fellow go, but I knew if he got one of those chickadees he would n't stop there. It was a case of either chickadee or shrike, and if you 're acquainted with birds at all you know which one you like best. As I returned to the doorway with the rifle, a sharp-shinned hawk struck the shrike and they both tumbled to the ground together. Abyssinian justice!

The quality of mercy was not strained that time. I'll admit it was merely a postponement, for a week later the little conqueror and his consort were sought out. They had murdered my pet phœbe, and the final act of their life-drama was closed.

Like the rest of us the sharp-shinned hawks sometimes experience failure, though so seldom that the occasion results in surprise; in one instance it caused bewilderment.

For twelve years I have tried by every known artifice to entice bluebirds into homes built for them. Promises of free rent, protection, abundant food, have all been ignored. Three years ago a pair inspected the chestnut mansions manufactured from the natural tree—bark left on, interior carefully finished with a chisel: in fact, all modern improvements except steam-heat! They stayed around two weeks, until I concluded they intended to take a lease. The captain of the outfit (do you know which one I mean?) gave special attention to the grape-arbor lure, going in and out dozens of times every day; and then, just as I was sure the couple was signing on for the season, with that feminine inconsistency not confined to birds, away she went to an old dead poplar with a deserted downy's home twelve feet up, out in the open valley. And, of course, *he* had to trail after! . . . No stamina!

Here one day in May, while I was watching the courting gyrations of a marsh-hawk, a sharp-shinned dived past and struck at the male bluebird. His feet hit the branch and his body knocked the intended victim over backward, thereby saving its life, for it recovered and found safety in the nest. Meanwhile, the little demon, scarcely larger than a robin, lit near by and was in the act of launching at the bluebird's mate when a pair of kingbirds tackled him with such vigor and determination that he actually cowered for a moment—the only time I have ever seen a hawk of this species exhibit the slightest fear. It may have been more surprise at the temerity of the fly-catchers than fright. Anyway, they certainly had his number!

Once a-wing, with his superior speed he soon outdistanced his pursuers, but the kingbirds hung on and made it interesting for him as long as they could.

## A BUFFOON IN BLUE

It was late October, calm with a soft haze and transcendent peace which falls upon our hills in that supernatural month: a day "when the spirit like a vision turns from cloud to forest, from changing tree to tree." I found a comfortable hemlock for a back-rest, in one of the small cañons near Chickadee Farm. This I utilized with the leisurely hope that a deer would wander down the runway, for a well-defined path had been trodden in the draw.

A gray squirrel appeared suddenly from behind a whitewood, scampered around through the rustling carpet a while, and ascended to its nest in a red-oak. Something was walking toward me; I heard the telltale scattering of crinkled leaves long before I could make out the identity of the traveler. Presently a pair of grouse appeared, strolling down the dried bed of the stream. They were not feeding—

simply out for a walk, enjoying, even as I, the color, quiet, and glory of the hour. At intervals they paused, shook out their feathers, wigwagged their splendid tails sidewise, and acted for all the world like Leghorn hens.

Opposite rose a sheer wall of haphazard rock one hundred feet high, crowned with stunted yellow pine. A blue jay emerged from the evergreens and began to descend silently and erratically, a few feet at a jump; but half-way down he stopped on a limb facing the wall and gave tongue. There was no uncertainty in his method of imparting some important information to any one within hearing. He spoke right out, withholding not a single thing that was on his mind.

Slowly and carefully my field-glasses were swung on the point of attack. And there it was!—savage head just visible over an edge of rock, eyes a cold, yellowish agate gray, opening half-way, then closing to a mere slit, indicating that old Busybody's scolding was getting beneath the skin.

As in "Alice in Wonderland," there it was—a cat's head planted on the ledge

This eye-flicker of impatience betrayed the enemy's presence. Without the binoculars' aid I think I should not have discovered him; even through the glasses his body with its red-brown spots was invisible against the red-brown leaves. As in "Alice in Wonderland," there it was—a cat's head planted on the ledge. And there it remained until I moved, when it disappeared as silently as a wood spirit. . . . A motionless wildcat crouched on a rock is so admirably camouflaged that the human eye seldom detects him. In over forty years afield I have discovered only this one, and my vision was directed to him by an excited jay, telling the forest all about it.

If we judged by the color of his coat, we should not be apt to place the jay in his correct place among feathered folk of the woods. But watch his mannerisms, and the answer is easier —half-brother of the crow. Taxonomically, the evidence is clear: the same heavy, blunt rounded bill; strong legs and feet; body skeleton almost similar, though of course much smaller. But any one familiar with the independent rascal would not have to study his internal structure for proof of his relationship to the shrewd old crow. In one respect, at least, the jay is the more advanced; he is forehanded. Individual crows do store away food when they find a surplus, but providence is not universal among them as it is with the blue jays.

Near our home, in the foot-hills of the Berkshires, two or three pairs raise families every year. Here they remain throughout the seasons. In winter we feed them, together with other cold-weather birds, not only because their beautiful blue is a cheerful note against the snow, but also for the jaunty indifferent air with which they play the game.

One cold morning last year a large ear of corn hung temptingly in the grape-arbor. In precisely nineteen minutes, every kernel—hundreds of kernels—had been carried away. How they pitched in! If birds perspire, that pair must have been wringing, notwithstanding zero temperature. They worked as hard as Mark Twain's jay which tried to fill a barn through a hole in the roof . . . until some of his mates, peeping in at the door, saw the acorns falling on the floor, hopped up into the trees, and gave him the laugh! These chaps of ours used more sense, in storing their plunder, than that benighted laborer.

I had been clearing out old dead chestnuts for years, and a few days after the incident of the corn I felled a ten-inch tree that still had some bark clinging to the trunk. I always remove bark, because the wood does n't decay one tenth so quickly if there is nothing to hold moisture. As I slid the ax lengthwise, out dropped several kernels of corn! Every chestnut cut down in that patch had one or more kernels tucked snugly away. I found some in holes where small limbs had rotted away on live-oaks and hickories. The nearest of these caches was five hundred feet from the grape-arbor. Of course there is no way of proving that our jays had carried all these away:

sequestering a quarter of the lot meant miles of flying—no lazy bird's job.

Some individuals of the human race like to assume the vestments and office of supreme judge over their wild kindred. Reams of printed testimony have appeared for and against any wild bird or animal unfortunate enough to have the spot-light of publicity flashed upon it. So it has come about at different times that the jay has been arraigned, and these printed words may start the argument anew. My only advantage, holding this brief, is that I am getting in the first word.

When our biologists at Washington undertake the study of a phase of life, they do so without sentiment, and the facts they present are cold, inescapable conclusions from which there is no appeal. Three quarters of the jay's food, as examination of the stomach proves, consists of vegetable matter, nuts, acorns, and small wild fruits; hard-shelled beetles, about four per cent.; grasshoppers, moth and butterfly egg clusters, caterpillars,

When a peering jay attempted to get a billful, there was trouble

and minor insects, about twenty per cent.; leaving one per cent. for birds' eggs, frogs, small fish, mice, snakes, and salamanders. Here is the case in a concise judicial brief. Verdict for the prisoner without the jury leaving their seats.

It is a safe rule to catalogue a loud talker among the bluffs and cowards. The jay would not be entitled to a nook in the hall of avifauna fame because of his courage, but that quality is not entirely lacking in his make-up. In some years the chickadees have called for their daily ration of suet as late as the middle of May. To supply this demand, a large piece of the delicacy was left in one of the cedar grape-arbor posts. A pair of catbirds, which had preëmpted a home site in the syringas near by, developed a fondness for the dainty. Catbirds, of course, eat spiders, bugs, and other forms of insect life; but here was an addition to their menu in which I had never known them hitherto to indulge. Evidently it was a rare treat, for they guarded the titbit most assiduously.

When a peering jay attempted to get a bill-ful, there was trouble. With feathers puffed out so they appeared like two slate-colored balls, the catbirds gave hot chase. Combined, they were too much for him. But the jay was n't going to let this opportunity go. He slipped out of sight and waited until only one guardian was visible. Then he came like a whirlwind. Before the catbird's mate could answer the frantic calls for reinforcements and reach the scene of action, the jay had seized a chunk of the booty and disappeared.

This campaign lasted over a week, until the last of the spoils had disappeared. The opening notes of battle never failed to call two interested observers to the windows.

I make no plea that the jay should be canonized among feathered saints. He has his faults,—yes, some which reach the ultimate wrong, murder, but this blood-lust is largely individual; and my belief is that only a small percentage gives way to it.

Last spring, about the time shad-bushes

spread their tents of white against the pale green of early May, a pair of jays selected a small hemlock seventy-five feet west of the house and began home-building. One line of approach was not visible from the porch where I sat, and they utilized it every time. Glasses were trained on the spot for minutes at a stretch, but the first glimpse would be of the bird at the nest with a billful of material.

They slipped through shrubbery ways as silently and deftly as a fox through the brush. After the young were hatched, I cut away interfering branches and watched the parents push food down those yawning yellow throats. A large gray moth was brought frequently. And I saw one of the parents tear a tent-caterpillar's nest to pieces; I 'm almost certain that some of the inmates were fed to the youngsters, though the distance was too great for me to be sure of this, even with six-power glasses.

While the blue-jay fledglings were still in the nest many regular leaseholders of Chickadee

Farm were building or had eggs in completed nests. A pair of chestnut-sided warblers were occupying the same briers in which they had resided the previous year. This was within fifty feet of the jays' home, and twenty-five feet from the southwest corner of our house. Chipping-sparrows, Maryland yellowthroats, song-sparrows, robins, phœbes, orioles, and cat-birds were all busy with family cares. Now, just so long as the jays kept unobtrusively to the western approach, they were completely ignored. But once or twice they ventured into the apple-trees. Instantly, vociferously, the allies gathered and chased the intruders away. Nor could I see that they had harmed a single home. Steal?—yes, but in the code of the wilds stealing is not listed as a crime: food is the finder's wherever he discovers it, and if the other fellow has n't wit enough to secrete it effectively, that is his misfortune.

Jays never become so tame as tree-sparrows or as chickadees. Caution is so pronounced in some that they never come to the porch feeding-

**Jays never become so tame as tree-sparrows or as chickadees**

tables. They perch in the near-by lilac bushes, watch the chickadees take a piece of suet, follow unobtrusively to see where it is hidden, and then quickly gobble it down, never making the slightest attempt to attack the smaller bird.

In the jays curiosity and teasing are strongly developed traits. Whenever you hear the alarm-notes (which do not require much imagination to translate into "Hey! Hey! *Here!*") investigate the cause. It is often interesting, as I found it in the case of that wild-cat.

North of our house about fifty feet there are two young black-walnut trees. When the nuts are nearly mature, red squirrels garner the harvest, carrying the large green husks with incredible ease along a snake fence to their cache in the hemlocks—each a miniature Hercules with the world in his teeth! While the squirrels are thus engaged in laying up the winter's provender the blue jays bother them not at all. But let one of the rufous-coated imps slip along the grape-arbor to the food-shelf to steal a bit of the chickadees' suet, and the jays are after him on the instant; and they will hover over him, sweeping, swirling, and scolding, until he reaches his evergreen shelter. Sometimes the attack is carried on with such aplomb, aggressiveness, and determination that defense becomes imperative. To stop even for a second is a tactical error, for the booty will be snatched almost from between the squirrel's jaws.

Many naturalists believe that birds and animals do not reason. John Burroughs, I think, was one of this group. Others are equally sure that they do. It seems to me this may remain always a debatable question because of the indefinite lines between instinct and reason. The blue jay's psychic capacity of distinguishing between kinds of food which the red squirrels were carrying (one they could not use and left alone, the other they wanted and went after) strikes me as being fairly close to reasoning. Here enters the personal element: just where does reason start and instinct leave off?

As with many other questions of life, the answer must be according to our individual point of view. I am not averse to admitting many of my wild feathered and four-footed friends to the reasoning grade. When we consider dogs, there is n't a fragment of doubt.

The jay's vocabulary is as distinctive as his dress. Most of our birds sing for a few weeks in the springtime and are almost silent the remainder of the year. Not so Mr. Jay! He talks throughout the twelve months, and every day, too. It is not all conventional conversation, either! Run into a flock of jays baiting an owl or a hawk, and you will hear the choicest assortment of Billingsgate ever uttered in the woods. Swear? My word! *No end!*

Their teasing sometimes turns out seriously. If you must tease, don't push it too far. Watch your victim's eyes. If these begin to grow hard, and the eyelids narrow like the gunman's in the Western yarn, forbear!—or the same thing may happen to you which happened to one of a crowd of jays annoying a broad-tailed hawk last spring. The hawk struck, and a member of the gang was lugged off to provide dinner for voracious little broad-tails.

After listening to the raucous scolding cries, it is difficult to believe that the mellow bell-like *pee-toe* note issues from the same throat. But it does; and it comes forth with a ventriloquist quality producing an effect of distance, making the call seem half a mile away when in fact it is uttered by a bird only a few yards off.

Like the crow, the jay has a great capacity for mimicry. His imitation of the wild *kee-ooo* of the red-tailed hawk is perfect, and seldom fails to deceive me. When I hear it, my eyes involuntarily turn skyward, for the sight of this hawk's majestic circles against the heavens is always alluring.

Facing the window where I write, is a hollow apple-tree with an aperture eight inches across, about ten feet from the ground. Every autumn a screech-owl takes up his residence therein. Sometimes he stays but a few days, sometimes all winter; but I am never in doubt

In a hollow apple-tree a screech-owl takes up his residence

about his arrival, because four or five of my vociferous friends the jays advise me that the little midnight prowler has returned to occupy the premises.

It is interesting to watch the air of utter indifference assumed by Mr. Yellow Eyes as he surveys the outlook, not bothering even to turn his head toward his aggressors. "Just wait until dark, you blue-coated ragamuffins!" he seems to say. "Maybe I 'll catch one of you asleep, and then . . ."

If the attack is pushed too far, he slips down into the hollow as quietly as a fade-out in a moving picture. When he vanishes, one of the boldest of his tormentors perches on the edge of the cavern for a moment and peers down. But there his courage stops; he ventures no farther.

When you really want to observe happenings in the woods, put on inconspicuous clothes, select a likely location, sit down, and *keep still.* I was doing precisely that in late April when a pair of jays alighted in an adjacent cedar. Usually you cannot keep still enough; they spot you almost every time; but the amorous urge seemed to dull the customary keenness of this particular pair, and apparently they did not know that I was watching. Could that series of soft musical notes come from the male's throat? It was almost unbelievable! Instead of the noisiest, most impudent creature of the woods, he was now the epitome of alluring persuasiveness. A plain case of feathered *Jekyll* and *Hyde*.

I have often wondered where our winter birds find haven when cold rain and sleet are abroad. One morning in late November when a southerly gale was driving great slants of rain across the hills and through the valleys, I remembered a sledge and wedge which I had neglected to bring down from the wood lot. It happened I had been cutting under a cliff. Glancing up at the squall-swept surface, I detected a bit of blue. And there were three jays snuggled together in a niche thirty feet up, well out of reach of the most violent gust, as comfortable as three human beings in a warm house. There I left them

—three rollicking buccaneers tamed by the elements to a condition in which they did n't even care to scold me! After all, is n't it those who, like ancient Greeks, take life's storm and sunshine with a laugh, that we most admire?

## PHILOHELA

NEARLY a century ago, according to our friend J. Cyprus, Jr., that queer animal the reformer was browsing around. True, the reformation undertaken in this instance was a minor one—revising "unworthy names." We wish, with all our hearts, that the large and blatant company of holier-than-thous would confine their attention to matters equally unimportant.

White, in his "Natural History of Selborne" calls the Woodcock "Scolopax," simply. Latham dubs him "Scolopax Rusticola." Wilson christens him "Scolopax Minor." This is, probably, the true patronymic of the American bird as he is a "minor"—a smaller animal than that described by the ornithologists of the old world. If you go to Delmonico's to eat out of season, you will ask for "la Becasse" and be mistaken for a Frenchman, and get a private room, and so, perhaps, avoid detection. Sportsmen generally among themselves talk of killing "cock"; but if they meet an old woman in the woods and want information where to beat, they ask her if she "has seen any blind snipes." A straggling boy will pocket your sixpence and send you up a rugged mountain on whose either side he will assure you there are "plenty of wood-cocks," and you will go and find after a weary travel, that you have had your tramp after *red-headed woodpeckers*.

Seeing, therefore, that the nomenclature is uncertain and sometimes undignified, reducing a much-valued visitor to the caste of a common dunghill chanticleer and, moreover, as this is the age of reform of unworthy names we propose to introduce to our readers the excellent subject of this article by his true title of "Scolopax Minor." . . . They have undoubtedly derived their family name from their cry—their Scolopaxian "Good-bye, I 'm off!" Anatomize the word and take out the vowels which when a bird is in a hurry he cannot be expected to have time to put in. Try it. "Sclpx!" The trail is out but is not the body of the sound perfect? . . . They are the only people who come to us with long bills whom we are particularly anxious to see. If any boy of theirs comes to us and says: "Here is your bill, sir!"—kick him out? We do not. . . . But as we have the right to pick our friends so we have to pick our birds; our enemy would say: "the first to the pocket the last to the bone."

Since William P. Hawes wrote his quaint and inimitable sketches (from one of which the above is quoted) our little brown-backed friend the woodcock has been more fortunate than many in the matter of names. His has been changed only once and he is now "Philohela"; appropriate enough, meaning a "lover of bogs" and less sketchy than Hawes definition of Scolopax.

March shook her skirts viciously, releasing from the folds a three-day blizzard which gave all animate things a terrific shaking up. The last pine in the valley, a splendid tree nearly two feet through, was twisted off and fell—fortunately away from the old farm-house. Two willows measured their length across the road, and many chestnuts dead on the stump found a last resting-place.

An enormous mass of rock, water, and frost had stealthily for uncounted years been separating from the main hill, and at last accomplished the task and added another jumble of rocks to those already below the cliff. And the birds! I don't like to think of them. The wild Nimrod of the storm was running amuck, waving Azrael on in his destruction. He made a thorough job of it: for weeks afterward I found their starved forms under bushes, in the woodshed, hidden in rock-crevices, even on the porch! Damn the old villain! If it had been possible to grab the Reaper by his indefinite neck, I should have wrung it surely.

Forty-eight hours later I was seated on the porch in a chair tilted against the clapboards, smoking contemplatively in the warm April dusk. Above the undulating blur of hills hung the stars, softly luminous through a gossamer haze. A gentle air wakened faint murmurs among the lilac twigs and wandered off. From the meadows the clear call of peepers. What is there in the simple notes so alluring? They are as characteristic of early spring, as much a part of it, as the changing willows or tesselated cottonwoods.

The little frogs paused, in that strange unanimous cessation of calls which comes now and then in their chorus, and into the interval drifted a single "*Scaip,*" then another, scarcely audible from the northern edge of the meadow. The woodcock, aristocrat of migrating game-birds, had returned! It was good to hear again its *sclpx* or *scaip*—whichever you choose; either is as near as letters can describe the sound. The note is similar to the night-hawk's and I remember my complete mystification in my early bird-studying days when I heard the call of a night-hawk in March on Long Island! I knew this aërial gymnast did not get here in that month, and searched the sky for the daring adventurer. No sight of him there! Moreover, the cry seemed to come from the ground. The puzzle soon was solved: as I advanced, a woodcock flushed and gyrated against the evening light, filling the dusk with continuous *scaips.*

Years ago that stretch of country north of Jamaica, Long Island, now called Forest Hill Park, was an unfrequented spot where my first enthusiastic delvings into the mysteries of wild life were made. Scattered through this terminal ridge of the island's backbone were many tiny swales perfectly adapted to woodcock occupation and I soon made the interesting discovery that the birds realized its advantages and were utilizing them. The knowledge that here, within the limits of a great city like Brooklyn, numbers of these fine birds followed through a large part of their life's cycle unmolested and, as far as I could tell, unknown save to me, was a secret I held close to my juvenile soul. Those were momentous days, when my first gun was aimed where it should not have been. The primitive was in the ascendant, but fortunately it soon succumbed in the battle with sentiment.

Here in this favored spot I learned that the woodcock did not confine themselves to bogs. True, the indications of their presence were more noticeable in the moist areas,—drill-holes and splatter,—but during the day they always retired to the dry ridges "forming down" among crinkled last year's leaves. Walk boldly through these upland covers, and probably you would fail to flush a single bird. Change tactics, move more slowly, pausing now and then if you suspected one was close by, and their natural nervousness would make them think they were watched, and soon the strain, proving too great, was released by flight. An odd reflex, exactly the opposite of that of nearly all other forms of wild life. By far the larger number of our furred and feathered friends are more excited by motion than the lack of it.

The woodcock menu is about ninety-eight per cent. angleworm, obtained by senses of touch and hearing. The extremity of the bird's long bill is prehensile, and so sensitive that it does not make the mistake of dragging out a root instead of a worm. Sight not being required for sustenance, the eyes are placed far back in the head, giving an owlish and extremely odd expression. With bill buried to the forehead in mud, birds with eyes forward would be seriously at a disadvantage, especially should an enemy approach from the rear. Arranged as the woodcock's eyes are, they could detect a prowling mink or fox in ample time for escape.

While this posterior location of the eyes increases the woodcock's range of vision on the ground, it is sometimes a handicap in flight. One October day a bird jumped a little way ahead. The gun flashed, but at that instant Big Eyes hit a birch limb and fell. Knowing it was not hit by shot, I picked it up in surprise and saw there was no indication of a wound on the soft brown plumage. As I held it the eyes opened suddenly. Only stunned. Searching my pockets, I found a bit of wire, twisted a couple of loose turns around one foot, and released the bird. In the light of present-day proof, through bird-banding, that many individuals return to the same locality year after year, there is nothing very remarkable in the fact that on the fourteenth of May of the succeeding year I flushed that bird from her family of four youngsters. But it was a pleased and astonished boy who held one of the downy chaps in his hand. They were the cutest little imps imaginable; with their short bills, and their bodies boldly striped lengthwise with black and pale yellow, they resembled exaggerated juvenile spotted sandpipers more than their mother.

Here I saw something that I was destined to note but once more in the following thirty-five years. Replacing the little tike among the leaves, I moved backward step by step, testing the distance I could detect its small form amidst the protecting environment. Ten feet . . . still clearly evident if I kept my eyes on it, but if my gaze shifted even a foot outside I had difficulty in recovering the motionless fuzzy ball.

Gathering her precious baby between her long toes, she was off

Fifteen feet . . . uncertain. Then, softly as an owl, the mother glided in, lit directly over her precious baby and gathering him between her long toes, was off. Back she came after the others, as silently as a spirit bird, transporting them to safety (at least as far as I was concerned). I pursued them no farther.

The day's happenings had filled the cup of interest to the brim: Balboa, when he scanned the illimitable Pacific, had nothing on me!

Few have thrown themselves more wholeheartedly into conservation and protection of wild life than Hornaday, but when he said the woodcock is extinct, I am afraid fear of what might happen was father to the statement. One trait which will postpone that evil day is the extraordinary wariness which seems to possess all woodcocks in certain years. Some autumns they will lie right under a dog's nose, refusing to fly until they are "kicked out"; other times, it is impossible to get within gunshot. This was notably so in the autumn of 1924. One of my hunting friends tells me he once scared out over a dozen in a patch about an acre in extent, and did not get a shot at one! Why are they "plain dumb" sometimes and at others wilder than grouse who have been hunted a month? Perhaps there is a kind of avian radio in the air. Figure it out if you can: it 's beyond me.

Most of us who wander afield are familiar with the ecstatic flight-song of the oven-bird, but how many have witnessed nocturnal hieroglyphics traced by Philohela against the dim evening sky?

The sun was gone. A clear white light, austere as that of a vestal virgin's lamp, filled the west. In the east, dusky steel blue merged into soft ashes of roses. Over the blurred distant hemlocks and near-by alders hung the pale segment of a new April moon. A sleepy white-crown greeted it with muted notes—"Oh, *dear, dear, dear!*"—as though complaining about its disturbed rest.

Where Otter Run joins the main brook I sat down on a maple trunk whose shallow roots in the tenuous ground had yielded to a norther the previous autumn, beneath three white birches. Although my resting-place was only a few hundred yards from the house, part of the trip was such hard going through the bogs as to make it seem three times the distance. Fortunately, black-flies were quiescent and mosquitos not numerous. A woodcock was near by, unseen, but betrayed by soft minor wing whistlings. Would he come into the open space in front? He would and did.

For ten minutes I watched a series of gyrations, pigeon-wings, and all the theorems of calculus combined, scarcely credible in a bird usually so staid and dignified. Up he went in spirals, twittering and cheeping, for fifty or sixty feet, at first clearly observable in the moonlight, gradually disappearing as he ascended, until only semi-musical notes told that he was still aloft. Down he came, pinions whirring, in a regular night-hawk dive (without the *boom*), sweeping off horizontally in a long slant to the ground. This side-slip brought him to rest on a tussock not fifteen feet away and I knew the primary reason for these wild stunts was somewhere near. There he strutted, tail perpendicular, head thrown back, bill buried in the breast feathers, *scaipping* every half-minute or so, his whole body jerking spasmodically at each call. I have no doubt his sweetheart thought him marvelous! —perhaps looked into his eyes even as females of a higher order have been known to look, murmuring, "Wonderful"!

While woodcock prefer clean alder- and willow-besprinkled meadows, they are by no means confined to such localities. I have frequently flushed them on hillsides from the tiny hollowed-out "form" where evidently they had spent the night—a simple tavern open to the stars and all wandering night winds. If such an elevated spot is selected as a nesting site, it is always within a short distance of proper feeding grounds—a hill lake or swamp to which the birds fly for meals.

Although gentle, quiet, unassuming, and

given strictly to minding their own business (humanity *et al.* please note!), they possess that most admirable of human virtues—high courage to an astonishing degree. Over Dover way a pair selected a spot directly between sled-tracks along which logs were hauled to the mill. The first time a pair of monsters dragging a tremendous juggernaut appeared, the female flew from her eggs, but thereafter when the horses passed on each side she merely crouched a little lower and sat tight while the swaying load rumbled overhead. How many humans would remain quiet if Ajax suddenly appeared driving a pair of brontosauruses ahead of a Gargantuan sled loaded with full-length trees? Would you crouch in silence and let this awe-some cavalcade thunder above you? Maybe, but it 's doubtful!

To me there has always been an air of mystery about the woodcock, and I never see one without hoping I may pick up something new in his life-history. Among materializations of this hope is the September day when I flushed twenty-three birds amid Yaupon-trees in sandy ground near Beaufort, North Carolina. What they were doing in that unsuitable environment, I cannot imagine any more than I can understand their presence in the salt meadows near Cape Romain, where the sloop's main boom, sweeping through the grass, scared them out as we shot down Ram's Horn Creek. It would n't surprise me to see them sauntering around on the lawn, but there is one place in which I really do not like to view them, and that 's a glass case!

Among the incidents in Mr. and Mrs. Big Eyes' career which is still shrouded in mystery is their method of feeding their young: do they accomplish it à la humming-bird—push the wiggling worm down the youngster's throat—or spread the dainty enticingly on a sedge table-cloth? Maybe I 'll find them at breakfast some day before the final curtain falls. I can discover no information about their table manners in any of our etiquette- or bird-books, can you?

## CHUCK LUCK

One hundred feet south of the porch, pale November sun shines on withered cornstalks in the garden. Of course they should have been cleared away and that sixth of an acre manicured against next spring. All farm magazines devote pages every year to instructions as to just how this should be done, but somehow I did n't get around to it. Even beanpoles stood in the ground. *That* is the last word in careless gardening!

Autumn had drifted in—calm, serene, beautiful. The days claimed and held me through hours of glowing forest color and skies of fathomless cobalt. Work? To the donjon-keep with the villain, ball and chain on each leg! Far better to lie a-hammock and

Leaning, listen to the listless crickets
Telling their old-time legend o'er again

And desultory bird songs from the thickets
Mingling regrets and warblings in one strain.

When the previous owner reclaimed this bit of wild woodland, he built a three-foot stone wall along the southerly edge, hauled loads of earth, and with his horses put in many days of hard labor. He believed he was making a garden! When I supplemented his efforts by blasting out a six-foot ledge in one corner I had the same idea in mind.

Well, that little cleared oasis is n't a garden, it 's a battlefield, and every spring hostilities are renewed. There is a wire fence around it, which helps a little. In this wild country, with insistent Nature forever poking her fingers against the back door, you could n't raise a flagpole without a chicken-wire guard. Park the brush-hook, sickle, or hoe for a day and the prolific Old Dame is right after any open space. The fence is covered now with masses of wild clematis, the seed-puffs of soft gray three inches across. Wild raspberry canes have intertwined, with complete indifference to the amount of work required to get them out, and quack-grass!—

But enough! If I got started on that, this yarn would be devoted to ravings against that arch-demon amongst weeds. The fight against rampant vegetation has been hard, but not entirely unsuccessful. A vigorous use of the hoe kept the enemy semi-subdued. The real scrap was with animated life, particularly as represented by members of the marmot family—in other words, H.S.M. Woodchuck. You won't have to do much mental exercise as to what "H.S.M." stands for—not if you have a garden where woodchucks abound.

I am of a complacent make-up and recognize the rights of other forms of life besides the human animal to live and enjoy themselves. On one hundred and thirty-five acres of prime A1 rock, woodland, and meadow the original inhabitants can do as they please. Foxes have left their footprints across the front doorstep; skunks have wandered casually around the porch; the broad wings of eagles have thrown their shadows on the roof; a pair of red-tailed hawks have built each spring a few hundred feet northwest of the house without any protest from me.

Even with the villains among birds and animals I have leaned backward on the side of consideration; but when one of them destroys in a single night as many beans as would keep two of us supplied for a week, then patience expires. The primitive instinct of self-preservation becomes dominant and the fight is on.

Carefully erected defenses, with wire turned out six inches at the bottom, proved effective for two years. I listened with a tolerant smile to tales of devastated gardens. "Nothing to it! Just lack of simple precautions!" etc. About mid-June of the third year, one morning when I went down to give the rows of growing vegetables their regular daily once-over, the blow fell—some solid crack, too! All young cabbages neatly beheaded—many not eaten, simply nipped off, tips laid alongside. Beans likewise, but the tender shoots devoured. Carrots ditto, although not entirely destroyed.

An hour spent with the sickle, outside the fence, revealed no hole, not a single break where a chuck could enter, yet the villain *was* a woodchuck: footprints in the soft soil revealed his identity plainly.

A steel trap is double-distilled anathema. If I lived in the far North, where tampering with another's trap-lines means a bullet, my existence would be abruptly terminated, for I take every trap I find. Shooting a fox or other animal is bad enough, but at least the end is swift. Catching it by the feet, holding it through bitter cold for hours,—yes, *days*,—is unthinkable: only the human animal could practise such cruelty. If there is a future existence, as far as my observation goes most animals are more entitled to immortality than many human atoms, and I believe that some of these same atoms will have a large host of ghosts to confront when they go west.

Here was an emergency: if the destruction

were not stopped our vegetable supply would be limited—and we are particularly fond of garden truck! If a snare were fastened to a tall stick so it could be seen above the bushes I could watch it virtually all the time, thus preventing needless suffering on the part of a victim. This was done, the loop carefully slipped down into a hole on the north hillside where the suspected wretch probably was lying doggo. The peeled wand stood upright all day. Either he was not in the hole or understood what that bit of line meant. At dusk it was still there and next morning the battlefield was strewn with more wreckage.

All right! In the matter of brains Mr. Woodchuck is considerably below the raccoon, and that grade of mentality was n't going to get to windward of *me*. With pipe and a twenty-five caliber rifle I sat down 'longside a convenient rock. In about half an hour the wire began to shake.

"Ah! that 's where you get under, is it?"

Wrong guess. Up he came, foot over foot,

as dexterously as a seasoned A.B., teetered a moment on top, changed ends, and backed down.

When hard pressed woodchucks will climb. I have seen them frequently among the limbs of low-branching trees, but they are of the ground, and, ninety-nine times out of one hundred make for a hole when threatened. Here was an individual capable of scaling wire fences, a feat I had never witnessed before. Extra rewards are supposed to come to those who are more clever than their fellows. In this instance it did n't work out. If *this* chuck, propped up on his haunches, surveying the prospect for an enemy before devastating the layout below, had been just an "ornery" chuck who tried to dig his way under the fence and failed, probably he would be on top of the earth now instead of under it!

The triple rôle of judge, jury, and executioner is not pleasant to one who loves the children of the wilds, especially when a creature is simply following the path of instinct and age-old habit, but there are times when it just cannot be evaded. This was one. Here and there old Dame Nature has dropped in amongst her family a murderer, a killer who destroys for the fierce delight he finds in slaying. When a sharp-shinned hawk grabs Mother Phœbe from the porch roof, lugging the ruffled mass of feathers off to her abattoir, the case is black enough, but add to this the atrocity of striking down one of your favorite song-sparrows and *leaving* it, fatally wounded, and the indictment is complete without further argument! That bandit must be extirpated!

Now, I don't mean to place woodchucks in this class. Maybe dragging real double-dyed villains into the picture is a sort of weak-kneed attempt to give the prosecuting attorney a little extra morale, a kind of smoke screen to cover the thin streak of remorse always following the act of blotting out sun and stars for any living thing.

Biologists tell us that the introduction of these fierce destroyers into the scheme of things is necessary in order to keep down superabundant life. In view of the fact that tragedy stalks close on the trail of *all* animated things, the statement loses force. A power omnipotent enough to bring the universe into being, and run it, surely could have arranged limited reproduction instead of encouraging overwhelming numbers kept within bounds by continuous destruction through more voracious forms. This may be questioning the wisdom of Omnipotence, but a Supreme Being formerly supposed to frown darkly and direct destroying rays at any human entity who dared question His methods is no longer *de rigueur*. It is even possible that He is not averse to being questioned; and although there may not be an answer, there is no evidence that interrogation hurts His pride.

Br'er Chuck is a conventional, staid old customer. His feeding schedule is about the same as ours—morning, noon, and evening. Along in the autumn, when laying on extra fat to carry him through the winter, he feeds any old time and becomes so stout that at a little distance bow can be distinguished from stern only by noting the direction in which he is going. Being a disciple of Lucullus may have its gastronomic advantages, but when a distended organ handicaps a fellow's speed enough to enable an enemy to catch him before the subway of safety is reached, of what avail the satisfied appetite?

After imitating the amiable Roman gentleman until it is physically impossible to crowd another atom of food within, Mr. Chuck stretches out on the warm rocks and nods in the drowsy October sunshine. At such times he is shrewd enough to remain close to a haven into which he jumps at the first sign of danger, emitting a sharp whistle as he disappears. Matter-of-fact as he is in most habits, an element of mystery enters into his home-building. Two years ago a cellar was dug in the hillside near the little town of Macedonia, a mile or so south of Chickadee Valley. A woodchuck burrow was encountered near the east side.

Twenty-five feet in it still continued: thirty . . . forty . . . The final measurement showed that gallery over fifty-five feet in length, turning around rocks, through sand, loam, and gravel.

What becomes of the excavated earth? At the entrance was perhaps a wheelbarrow load; at the exit only a trowelful. There are two possible answers to this query: the earth is either carried out and scattered some distance from the entrance or packed along the sides as the burrow is dug. The latter seems most likely, but how the creatures do it is puzzling. Try digging a hole with a crowbar and see how far you 'll get; then imagine driving a five-inch hole fifty-five feet, compressing the earth along the sides. There 's a catch in it somewhere. Of course the length of this tunnel was extraordinary, the average being from five to ten feet.

Many casual and some keen naturalists tell us the chuck always has an exit to his den which he uses to escape when attacked below-ground. Suppose we get at the facts here. When Bethman-Hollweg asked if England considered the terrible results to follow her entry into the World War, Earl Grey answered, "Fear of consequences never deterred England from upholding her solemn word." I believe Grey's ethics correct, so here goes:

In fields or ground where digging is easy it is true there are sometimes one or more exits, but in woods or on these rocky hillsides it is not so. I have found many burrows with entrances only and am convinced that extra openings are added solely for Mr. Chuck to duck into when outside, or for ventilation. There is no animal in this part of New England with sufficient temerity to tackle a woodchuck in his den. I once saw a chuck dive to safety a few jumps ahead of a mink. Did the pursuer go in after him? He did not!—just sniffed disappointedly at the mouth of the hole and went on. Sometimes foxes make half-hearted attempts to dig woodchucks out, but a single instance where this has been accomplished successfully has never come under my observation.

I am aware that I stand virtually alone on this point, but that cannot be helped: we must record happenings as we see them. It must be understood that I refer to full-grown animals: neither mink nor weasel would hesitate for one instant to tackle a young woodchuck.

While iconoclastic bricks are in the air let 's shy one at another myth:

In a beauty show the chuck would take no prize; nevertheless the unprepossessing old chap owns the distinction of being the only animal in North America who has had a day named after him. On the second of February he is supposed to awaken and if the sun is out so he sees his shadow, he goes back into his hole for forty days more of winter sleep! Now, how ever did that story originate? If you awakened from sound slumber and found sunshine and warmth without, naturally you would conclude spring had arrived or was just around the corner. You 'd sit up and wait for it, would n't you?

That 's just plain sense. Yet this ancient tale persists year after year, with its illogical cross-eyed conclusion.

Vulcan or whoever had the contract for building these Taconic Hills celebrated the completion of the job by having a game of jackstraws with the rocks, leaving them in every conceivable formation. One day I stepped around the end of an upright slab of granite north of the house and cornered old Graybeard in the apex of an acute triangle, my boots forming the base. He rose on his haunches—it was two feet from the ground to his wrinkled nose—and faced me courageously.

"Old Bean, I 've long wanted a chance like this: will you behave and listen a few minutes?"

He chattered his teeth, the two big front ones a pair of wicked chisels: "All right! Make it snappy!"

"I just wish to remark that as long as you keep on this side of the fence and away from the garden, you and I shall be friends, BUT . . ."

"Yes, I know! If I go nosin' around down

there, I'll get caught in one of those iron things with snapping jaws. . . . So you 're the muttonhead who murdered my brother? You look as if you had some kindness, but I guess not. . . . No soul!" He re-chattered his jaws and continued: "Say, who owns this country, anyway? You came here a few years ago and started in telling us who have been around for thousands of years, just what we must or must not do."

"Wrong, old Gray-top! Your original habitat was the woods. Why don't you stay there instead of edging out into the fields? You were n't bothered much by man as long as you remained in the forest. Besides, I have to live as well as you, and all I 'm asking for is one sixth of an acre—*one sixth of an acre*; do you get that? You can have all the rest of the world as far as I 'm concerned, so I don't see where you have any legitimate growl coming. How about it? North of the house or fight?"

"Oh, all right! North of the house goes! Just step to one side so I can pass you; my hind legs are tired. . . . Thank you. Good-by." I saw him several days later feeding on a viburnum root, surrounded by an inquisitive group of Leghorns.

"Making out pretty well, are n't you? Don't find it much of a hardship to live up to your agreement? You 'd better continue to keep it, too, or I 'll sic my fighting humming-bird at you!"

"Don't do that! I 'm afraid of him. . . . Yes, I 'm making out all right. I really don't *need* young cabbages, but we think we want everything we 're told we can't have. . . . Any of you two-legged animals like that?"

"All of us!"

Two years ago last spring a little black-and-white dog adrift in town placed its paws on the running-board of a friend's car, pleading to be taken in. It was. The rescuer possessed three dogs, so ownership was transferred to me. Pal never would take a blue ribbon, because it would be difficult to select any particular breed under which to enter her. Three strains are evident: coach, wire-haired, and fox-terrier. Perhaps an expert could detect half a dozen more. However, lack of pedigree didn't prevent Pal's entrance into the game of keeping down the woodchuck population with wholehearted alacrity and enthusiasm. A dog soon learns respect for the courage behind that pair of daggers in the front of a chuck's jaw, but usually gains his experience at the cost of many severe slashes. Some dogs never learn and return from a chuck fight looking as though some one had spilled a can of vermilion paint over them.

Pal developed a technic of attack entirely original, and in twenty recorded battles (and probably as many more fought in the woods) she received only two small bites.

Her first two victims were small, their existence terminated by shaking. The third affray was with the reprobate who specialized in green peas. We caught him one morning in the act of hauling down five-foot vines with his front paws so he could get at the tender tips.

To and fro over his back went the dog, the chuck trying to follow with his head, but his reactions were too slow. In a few minutes these attempts to follow Pal's rapid movements seemed to confuse him. The dog sensed this instantly as she went over, reached for, and got, the fatal neck hold.

As long as there is the sightest resistance Pal attacks furiously, but when she realizes her antagonist has taken the count, interest ceases and she pays no more attention than to a clod of earth.

Old Graybeard disappeared before the dog's advent. What happened to him I do not know. If he went out on the Long Trail, it was none of my doing. I am rather glad he *is* gone, for if the game old boy had chanced to mix it with Pal the scrap would have been a fierce one. Besides, I had promised that patriarch he would not be molested, and am I not my dog's keeper?

Old Graytop was feeding on a viburnum root, surrounded by an inquisitive group of Leghorns

## COONS OF CHESTNUT CAVERNS

A YEAR or so ago a light snowfall came in the first part of December, and I went up to see if regular tenants had taken possession of the chestnuts. They had! The telltale blanket showed a maze of tracks which at a cursory glance seemed to indicate a full regiment of racoons abroad beneath that tree the night before.

Thirty minutes of careful examination revealed the fact that this intricate lacery had been made by five, certainly by not more than seven, of the nocturnal prowlers. There were the slender prints, nearly two inches long, of the older ones, intertwined with slightly smaller footprints of maturing children. Red- and gray-squirrel tracks were numerous: the "old homestead" evidently was occupied by a variety of lodgers.

The temperature rose, the sun climbed higher along its shortened arc across the southern rim of the earth. Perhaps the warm morning might tempt one of the night wanderers out for a glimpse of the bright world? A gray squirrel appeared within ten minutes; these are impatient little fellows and usually show themselves in a short while if the winter's day is mild. Not so old Smarty Coon! For more than an hour I watched that hole, where a four-inch limb had decayed, and concluded the family were all sound asleep. Then my vigil was repaid.

My eyes left the dark orifice for only an instant; but when they swung back, the color of the circle had changed to pale, dull yellow with a traverse band of black. Now began an endurance test. Who would move first? Of course, I did! Instantly, Mr. Sharp Eyes faded within his retreat. I am quite sure he spied me the moment he looked out, and had been contemplating this strange object all the while.

"A comfortable winter's sleep to you and your family!" I said. "I 'll be around later to see if everything is all right, and along in early spring I 'll collect the rent!"

Do not think I meant to catch any member of this little family and sell its pelt! If complacent femininity (or self-satisfied masculinity) wrapped in coonskin coats, depended upon me to supply those fashionable garments, they would freeze or dress in wool. The indifference of those who adorn themselves in furs of slaughtered wild folk is amazing. Either they must be ignorant of the ghastly methods used in procuring the material, or they are hardened to suffering.

No, that was n't the way I intended to play landlord. I meant to trace out part of my tenants' habits and ways of living, and tell the story with pen and brush—a rather vicarious way of collecting rent, but effective and, besides, not at all annoying to the lessee.

Our chestnut-trees, with their caverns sometimes inhabited by such interesting denizens, attracted me when, thirteen years ago, we left urban ways—forever, I hope!—for this spot about eighty miles north of New York City. The first spring of our residence here showed many live chestnut-trees, but the blight had even then got its strangle hold upon them all. No other trees in our New England forests possess so many good points; for general usefulness they stand alone. Split rails of chestnut endure fifty years; a natural—not sawed—stick set in the ground outlasts all others, possibly excepting cedar.

To allow these hundreds of dying trees to go completely to waste would not do, so the bid of one of my neighbors was accepted, and a fifty-four-inch circular saw soon shaped them into ties and general lumber.

"I see you have n't cut that big fellow, a quarter of a mile west of the house," I remarked; "nor that old giant to the northward! Too big to handle?"

"Never saw a tree in this country too big for me to tackle," he replied. "Those two old boys are hollow, and though they measure six feet through, I would n't get enough out of either to pay for the work."

Unlike other deciduous trees, a large chestnut will stand for many years after life has left it. The roots decay very slowly, perhaps because of the presence of tannic acid in unusual quantity. The supporting network of another tree will disintegrate in a year or two and the trunk will fall. It was eight years ago that the last nut dropped, the final leaf fluttered earthward, and life departed from our chestnut-trees, except in the small shoots; but my two old warriors still lift sturdy arms, and probably they will defy the elements for years to come. I hope so, for they are the two largest and most popular apartment-houses on the place!

The hill tree stands on what was a buckwheat field many years ago. The flat rock on which the grain was threshed with flails is still above-ground, but birches have overgrown the area. Looking at it now, it is difficult to understand how a plow ever turned that soil. A little distance southward a brook wanders among the rocks, turning and tumbling, always intent upon finding the easiest way down-hill. Near by is one of those old stone fences, four feet at the bottom, three feet wide at the top, and three high, both sides and top slanting inward. The average of these stone walls lasts perhaps seventy-five years; this one has already reached that age, and looks good for another century. The men who built these rough monuments are gone. Hereabout, fifty cents a rod was what they received, and one of the last of the genus told me that it was considered nothing remarkable to lay up eight rods a day. . . .

A subsequent visit to my little tenants made it clear to me that the old folks had driven the youngsters out, or had allowed them to depart of their own volition. One new home was established in a dying maple some distance away, another on a rocky ledge. Next old Bar-face himself was dismissed, and evidently was informed in no uncertain terms that a long journey would safeguard his health. His trail led to a cave in a jumbled group of rocks over a mile away. A most important event in the old lady's life was n't far off, and she did n't intend taking chances with a father's jealousy. (Positive evidence of the male's cannibalistic propensity is wanting, but twice I have found young, dead from exposure, at the foot of trees where probably they have been evicted from the nest by the father.)

Along about the time Old Sol crossed the equator, four little blind racoons wiggled around on their comfortably lined bed in the cavern's warm darkness. The winter days of alternating hibernation and awakening were past for the mother. Four long-nosed and insistent mouths meant that plenty of food was necessary for her if they were to be well nourished. An early April moon hung low above the serrated hemlocks in the southwestern sky, a thin segment giving barely enough light to show a strong, sturdy figure making its way to the ground. Cleverly as she handled her feet, the task was not an easy one, for in places the rough bark was gone and the smooth weather-seasoned wood offered slight foothold. After many twistings the ground was reached and the feel of good solid earth impelled her to give two or three exuberant jumps—exactly like a cat at play.

The winter had been mild, with little snow, the near-by brook gossiped in undertones instead of roaring noisily as when it has to carry a foot or two of melted snow from the hills. From the little meadow above came no shrill piping of peepers, but half a mile below, in the broad marsh between the main ridges, she could just detect their high, insistent notes. That was a long journey; she would defer it until later and to-night would see what could be found nearer home. She paused, sniffing eagerly among the leaves. Then her powerful front paws went into action: grass, earth, and leaves flew aside, and an inch-long fat white grub was seized in the sharp little teeth, carried to the brook, carefully washed, soused again and again in the cold water, then—and not until then—daintily eaten.

It was but a morsel, and eased the hollow feeling in her stomach not at all. A dozen more grubs were excavated, the same rinsing given every one. Then she transferred her attention to the banks of the stream. Here she found better hunting. Several newts and salamanders were dug out of their hiding-places under stones, and by the time the moon had set, a satisfactory amount of food had been stowed away and she started for home.

Absolute silence met her return. Young as the children were, the instinct to utter no sound or make any movement, until no danger threatened, was fully developed. Only when she nuzzled their tiny forms did they emit little squeals of greeting, quickly squirming around until each was in a position to get a late dinner or an extra-early breakfast.

Food became more abundant as spring advanced, but it was more difficult to catch. Constant persecution will teach meadow-mice, chipmunks, and even salamanders, wariness, and before long the supplies of the neighborhood had dwindled or disappeared ere old Ma Coon could pounce on them.

So one night in May, when the full moon was abroad, she determined to forage and make a trip to the lower meadow, where she still heard the high-pitched notes of the peepers. She did not intend to waste time hunting them —too small!—but mingled with their call was a deeper one, the full bass boom of the bullfrog. The hind legs of one of these fellows would furnish as much meat as twenty peepers, so why bother with the small fry?

A quarter of a mile through the woods, then she stepped out into the open road, sniffing the air a moment for possible danger, the lustrous moonlight revealing her compact body covered with long dusky-brown hair, balanced by a tail nearly as long, its black rings clearly visible. The head, long and pointed and keen as a fox's, the characteristic black mask across the eyes, gave her an air of sagacity, shrewdness, and capacity to take care of herself in an emergency. Nor are these phrenological indications misleading; the racoon is an individual, a personality, among the folk of the wilds. She was not a graceful walker. Each foot came down flat, a plantigrade. Now, running—that 's a different thing! The tips of her feet hit the ground so lightly they scarcely seemed to touch at all, and carried her forward a thing of light grace and speed. In movement, one moment a miniature bear, the next an exaggerated mink.

The bank on one side of the stream through the meadow was high and firm; on the other it was virtually no bank at all, the water spreading out over the flats. Several old rail line fences extended into these acres of black mud and crossed the brook. Jumping to the top of a rail, where it left the dry ground, the coon ambled along. Where this fence reached the brook, one end of the lower rail had slipped out of the post-socket and lay slanting in the water. Here she crouched, her nose almost submerged.

In the lore of the wilds, a correct synonym for patience would be *life.* This wise old mother knew that many a time when younger she had been too impetuous. Minutes went by; the shadows of near-by willows enveloped her. It would have taken a keen eye to see anything alive on that log, half hidden in the water. An hour passed, when suddenly two great protruding eyes appeared within four inches of her nose. A motion swift as conjuring, and a gleaming bit of white rose from the water, landing on the far bank. The dark bulk of the racoon followed so quickly that the two bodies hit the ground almost simultaneously. Had the frog lit on his feet, he might have had a slight chance, but falling on his back as he did, he was doomed. One snap, and life for him was over! The front and hind legs were carefully detached, the rest of the body discarded. After the inevitable washing, both front and one hind leg were eaten on the spot, and with the other titbit in her teeth, Ma Coon started for home.

The extreme caution of the blind stage of the youngsters had disappeared; they had learned to recognize the sound of their mother's claws as she ascended. To-night, two eager faces in the doorway greeted her return with impatient little mews, half grunt, half squeal. The attempt of the most impetuous to seize the food was met promptly with a sharp cuff. The morsel was equally divided, and a portion given to each. It was by no means a full meal for those growing young appetites, but a pleasant wrangle over the bones diverted the babies' attention from their stomachs. With all the intensity and passion of four little bear cubs they fought over the prize until they chewed it up.

Imperceptibly at first, then more rapidly, the summer nights lengthened, and Mother Coon undertook the task of teaching the young ones to leave the nest and descend to the ground. This too called for patience, and although occasionally she lost it and boxed the laggard's ears, on the whole she showed more forbearance than many a human parent. Early one morning the most venturesome infant crawled out and started down backward, while the anxious mother watched from a near-by crotch. Absence of bark prevented the little explorer from getting a real hold with his tiny claws. But he succeeded. Coon see, coon do! The rest tumbled out, one after another.

Still under parental direction, the youngsters began foraging for themselves. One of them, coming suddenly upon a water-snake in a shallow pool, frightened the brown-ringed reptile into releasing a trout held crosswise in its jaws. Searching little pools isolated by receding waters of the brook, they caught numbers of marooned trout and chub. Now, if you are a fisherman, do not go up in the air over this! Those fish would have died anyway.

This easy living aroused in one an independent spirit which led him to occupy a little cave some distance from his birthplace, and to start a home of his own. Another, following the main valley brook one night, reached a place on the bank where the grass had been trampled flat, a spot strewn with trout heads and tails. Here was a find! And the discoverer proceeded to enjoy it voraciously.

It was one of the times when she regretted the necessity of washing each bit. The performance cramped her speed, and she may have neglected one or two pieces. Turning in the midst of her Gargantuan gorging, she saw two intense eyes watching from the alders. In the next instant, a regular old grandfather coon advanced from the thicket.

"Don't you know you 're poaching?"

"What 's that?" she asked.

"You 're stealing my fish! I live in that chestnut over there on the edge of the marsh, and this is part of my hunting-ground. Get off, and don't ever come back, you thief!"

Argument with a gentleman of his weight and belligerence would have resulted only in a good licking, so she hesitated not at the order. She retreated swiftly, nor paused to give even a tiny snarl. However, the meeting proved of value, inasmuch as she learned one of the primary lessons of the wilds. You must find an unoccupied hunting-area, post it as yours, and keep intruders off.

Grandfather may have had his suspicions, but the young lady did not know that this spread had been provided by a pair of otter for their own family. What they discarded were merely the crumbs from the table of the lord of streams. Otter and Grandfather Coon may have met at the banquet board, but there had been no serious difference, for the impressionable ground showed no marks of battle. Courageous but no fool is "the little brother to the bear." Grandfather was far too wise to mix matters with such an antagonist. A single blow from an otter's front paws would have been enough.

Grandfather Coon's residence in the fantastic old chestnut is about five hundred feet north of our house. It has been occupied more

The anxious mother watched from a near-by crotch

or less regularly for twelve years by gray squirrels and racoons. Each family, apparently, keeps to its own side of the tree and they get along in friendly fashion. It overlooks the full sweep of lowlands clear to Peaked Mountain, two miles north, and therefore is a favorite tarrying-spot for many kinds of hawks. I have seen redtails frequently leave its lofty limbs in slanting drop for woodchuck or rabbit, marsh-hawks and crows use it to rest upon, and occasionally that gray terror the goshawk perches on one of its arms.

One morning, while breakfasting and watching the slow November dawn coming through the southeastern notch, I saw a large bird appear in the wan light. It was almost as large as a crow, but with glimpses of white. It approached, flying, across the lower edge of the orchard, with the characteristic dipping flight of the woodpecker. My thoughts flashed back thirty years to the austere winter hills of Maine. A pileated woodpecker!

Alighting on one of the hollow limbs of the

old chestnut, he sounded his *rat-tat-tat.* How it did ring across the valley! Grandfather Coon was accustomed to the tiny taps of downy and hairy woodpeckers, but this machine-gun volley was something new. Through the field-glasses I saw the astonished face at the opening, looking at the splendid drummer only a few feet away.

"Surprised you, old fellow, did he? You 're not alone!"

Three decades is a long span, but that jaunty red-cockaded head brought back the spruce pinnacles against the wide blue . . . smoke as motionless above the cabin chimney as the tingling frost-suffused air . . . the hoarse call of moose in the tamarack, when the hills of Maine held my willing feet!

Most of the men and dogs who tramped these woods at night have gone west. My neighbors are given to following the golden rule; they know I do not want them to destroy wild life on these acres, so they abstain. Hereabout, it is many years since racoons have been treed by dogs, then shot out of limbs. Relieved of this menace, they have thrived, and I believe right now there are as many of the little semi-rascals as the land will support.

How sport enters this game of galloping over rocks for the best part of the night for a chance to blow a harmless bunch of fur out of the treetops, I cannot and never could comprehend. I went coon-hunting once. In the hills by the little town of Alfred, Maine, four of us, a dog also, circled around until two in the morning, before the pup came to anchor at the foot of an old stump some thirty feet tall in a small clearing.

"Here 's a big 'un—no doubt of that!" We could easily discern its elephantine contour against the starlit sky.

"We 've only got this twenty-two caliber pistol. If I miss him he 'll go into the brook and we 'll lose him!"

"I 'll go back and get the gun," said Frank. Back he went, two miles, whilst we important Nimrods, the dog also, talked loudly beneath the roost for over an hour. Then the armed traveler returned.

"Here, put that lantern behind something."

The gun was aimed, exploded; the animal came clawing to the ground.

"Don't let him kill the dog!"

"Hey, look out! You banged my foot!"

"Stomp on his head!"

The deed was done, the lantern brought. A large Maltese tame wildcat lay at rest within the circle of light.

"Well I 'll be dashed!"

And I hope I shall be if I ever go on another coon-hunt. The first was plenty, and it will be the last.

Although the tenants of our two old monarchs and their confrères are no longer persecuted by their most serious enemy, dog and man, they are not immune to "the bright face of danger" besetting all wild life.

Half a mile west of the hill tree the brook wanders along for a hundred yards for almost a level stretch. Fine oaks and whitewoods arch

A slanting drop for woodchuck or rabbit

thickly overhead, dimming the light. Wild ginger carpets the black, damp earth. A place of cool shadows where I always linger. On one of the sandy banks built in the spring by the torrential brook I came upon evidence of a terrific battle. The signs were not difficult to read. A mink and a coon had engaged in a furious struggle, and neither had won, because both combatants had lacked the strength to bring it to a lethal conclusion.

The racoon's capacity to stand off one of these bloodthirsty demons is due not only to his dauntless courage but also to the fact that he fights primarily with his head, supplemented by teeth and claws. He is a furred strategist. His long, rough, hairy coat is unquestionably an important factor in his favor, preventing an antagonist from easily gaining the fatal throat hold.

I tracked the plucky old fellow to a hollow poplar, offered my silent admiration and the hope of a speedy recovery. The mink had holed up a little way below; I gave him slight sympathy and hoped old Azrael would get him. Widely divergent wishes presented to animals whose characteristics were accidents of birth. Looked at in this light, it seems scarcely fair, but it 's the way we 're built; we cannot help hating a gratuitous murderer, or admiring courage.

Out of seven dead weasels, two were killed by racoons. The antipathy between weasel and coon is strong, and although I have never seen an actual contest, it is probable, I think, that the coon makes short work of this miniature edition of his larger brown-coated relative, the mink.

As September drifted into "the haunted month," Grandfather Coon became restless, wandering farther afield. One early October night, his impatient feet carried him several miles from home territory. Padding along in a woodchuck trail, he came suddenly to the bank of a small lake, where the warm glow of sunrise was reflected—a ruby set in yellow birch-tree gold. A convenient fallen trunk extending obliquely into the water offered his favorite resting-place. Crouching low, his pointed nose an inch above the surface, he waited for breakfast. The warm sun felt comfortable. The night had been close to frost. His eyes narrowed . . . almost asleep. Then convulsively he drove sharp claws of all four feet into the tree trunk; something was yanking with persistent force at the end of his tail!

He turned his head and looked into the cold, malignant eyes of a monstrous snapping-turtle. His hind legs were slipping, and then the terrific strain was so suddenly released that the reaction almost threw him into the water on the other side. The merciless jaws that never release a hold had caught only the fur, not the end of his vertebræ.

While his fascinated eyes still stared into the basilisk orbs set in that horrific head, he saw a black hole appear in the forehead, heard the sharp snap of a rifle. His gaze shifted to the figure standing close by in the brush: that was not an enemy. He had seen a similar shape many times near the old home tree, and walking back along the trunk he moved sedately past, and was saluted with a wave of the hand.

"Lucky for you, old boy, that he had you only by the hair, and twice fortunate for me that I happened to be right here. For the past three years that arch-devil has destroyed everything in this lake that he could get that vise of his on. He ate up a whole family of wood-ducks this spring—mother, father, and all the babies. Thanks for your assistance as bait. Good hunting to you, and a pleasant ramble!"

Although dead, these two majestic sentinels of a dying race still rear their gaunt limbs aloft, loving the wide air and sky too well to hear the call of earth. There they are, one on the hill, one overlooking the intervale, their bare arms outstretched against the gray December clouds, their stout sides still protecting the lodgers who never will be compelled to appeal to the courts about increased rents while I am their landlord!

# DOCTOR LOGCOCK AND COMPANY

## I

The tree trunks forming the old corduroy tote-road were almost gone; in fact, where the ground was moist they had melted entirely into the earth. In some stretches tamaracks, birches, or alders encroached so thickly it required a woodsman's eye to trace the path. The men who had built and hauled lumber over its corrugated surface were gone, too—a hardy, indomitable race who handled that tool of empire, the ax, as easily as most of their descendants would a willow slip.

October had just released the hand of September, but already in these northern Maine ways the frost-spirit had been abroad o' night, painting the deciduous trees along the edges of the lake with varying soft, exquisite shades

—pale yellow, deep topaz, mauves, and browns, with touches of Tyrian purple.

"Any of the boys left who put this way through, Jo?"

"No."

"What 's become of Bronson?"

"I 'll show you a little farther on."

As we turned north the forest changed from a tapestry of many colors to the deep, dark, alluring green of spruces. Ahead loomed one of the few remaining giant pines and, coming abreast of it, I saw a small, rough wooden cross at its broad base.

"Four of us came in last year; Bronson was one of the guides. When we reached camp about dusk he was n't with us. I went back and found him against this tree, gone out as quietly as a falling leaf."

The man whose name was cut in rude letters on the crossed sticks was as much a part of the forest as the tree beneath which he rested. His spirit did not have to break through the four walls of a room to start on the long trail, but slipped off, on the great adventure, among the things he had loved beyond all else. Somehow I think the long traverse would lose some of its uncertainty if we could all start that way.

We reached the little cabin tucked away in the wilderness, fifteen miles from anywhere, a little after noon. *Anywhere*, did I say? Not exactly that, for around it were clustered many of the real things that lured us back year after year.

Jo looked about him. "Everything seems to be here except a wash-basin. You start the grub and I 'll soon fix that."

Jo took his ax, a short-handled, keen-edged three-pound instrument, cut off a section of spruce from one of the logs stacked against the side, hollowed it out neatly, and in ten minutes came in with a good substitute for the lost article. Fascinated, I watched him handle that tool; every stroke counted; not one was wasted. There were many generations of pioneers behind his dexterous hand.

We spent the afternoon scouting for moose signs. Jo was a hunter and probably always would be one, although even in him I detected, each time we met, a distinct lessening of the destructive tendency. For me the glamour of the chase had long since faded. Camera, brush, and vision had displaced deadly weapons. Years ago a wounded grouse had swung my wavering allegiance to the gun away from it forever. I hope the pain and question in his splendid eyes as they closed will not haunt me on the other side of the Divide.

Against the clear amber light the trees deepened from dusky green to black. In the pale rose of the southeast, Sirius twinkled, a blue-white diamond calling into light the lesser suns of rubies and sapphires. Then into that quiet came the clear, poignant notes of a white-throat repeating, as in a dream: "Oh, clear, clear, clear, clear!"—its crystal spring-song, intensifying rather than breaking the silence, so utterly did it merge into the spirit of the hour.

They bedeviled him so persistently that he fairly frothed at the mouth

Long after the platinum segment of the western moon had dropped behind the spruce spires we sat smoking, talking of many things, by the beguiling camp-fire. At last the sandman's touch prevailed; we wet down the fire and turned in.

In more ways than one dreams are inexplicable phenomena and not the least mysterious thing about them is the fact they often have no connection with recent thoughts or happenings. In the heart of the Maine woods why should I have dreamed that I was jumping from tree to tree in the depths of an African jungle, pursued by gorillas shooting at me with automatics? The gorillas, apparently, could not climb, while *I* was an adept at that game. My yells for help disturbed Jo, for as I awoke and saw him looking at me in the dim light the sharp barks of the pistols continued.

"That 's only old Log-roller tapping outside for breakfast."

"Tapping? You call that *tapping?*"

"Sure! We fed him last winter and he 's back again. Forgot to tack up the chunk of suet I lugged in for him. It 's daylight; might as well turn out now we 're awake."

When I opened the door and stepped out into the clear morning air the pileated woodpecker flew from the cabin to a dead tree, sidled around back of it, peering inquisitively, his flaming head a vivid patch against the black-green conifers. When Jo appeared with the suet, the bird came fearlessly around into full view. Whether he recognized the difference between us, I don't know; but I 'm inclined to think it was the glimpse of food which emboldened him.

Jo placed it under an old wire kitchen sieve while the woodpecker, ten feet above his head on the tree, watched as he fastened it securely and stepped back several paces. Then, backing down in a series of short hops, the bird went after breakfast like an April bear, tearing out chunks as large as could be dragged between the interstices of the screen. In a few minutes his mate appeared, but she was much shyer, refusing to participate in the spread until we had retreated some distance.

"That 's a three-pound piece of fat, and you can see how long it would last without the wire! Last year I had five pounds: it was later than this, along in November, and the camp-robbers had come down from the north. Between them they cleaned it up in three days! They 'd have done better than that if the last of it had n't been hard to get out through the grating."

Our supply lasted, owing to the absence of Whisky Johnnie (one of the many names for our friend the camp-robber) over a week. The morning after it was finished I trailed the male until noon. During the five hours he lit on one hundred and sixty-three different trees. Most food was obtained from the dead gray or white birches, two short-lived species of trees. On one stump he remained sixteen minutes, tearing off large sections of decayed wood and flaying the papery bark off in sheets. It was a thorough, workmanlike job of demolition, and when it was completed the ground was littered with the debris for yard's around. It was absorbing to watch this black-white-and-red dynamo in action, and although he was but a dozen feet above the earth, there would frequently be a sliver of bark in the air before the preceding one had reached the ground.

Sound evergreens attracted slight attention, as they offered few lurking-places for grubs. Two spruces hit by lightning and rapidly dying were carefully inspected on the sides where the bark had been slivered off in long strips. Small acorns, eaten whole, rounded out the insectivorous menu. About noon he disappeared into the large-mouthed cavity of a poplar—perhaps for his midday siesta! for in the half hour I waited he did not venture a single inquisitive peek.

In flight the logcock is a conspicuous figure, the white markings beneath flashing in regular sequence as the wings open on the rise, close on the drop of the characteristic looping woodpecker curves. Sometimes these parabolas are accentuated almost to segments of circles, and accompanied by chuckling calls. Imagination does not require much encouragement to picture an old hen flying overhead.

All of us experience some happenings which linger so tenaciously in our subconscious minds that they recur again and again, without effort of memory to revive them. Moonlight on the sea, glory of autumn, starshine on quiet waters —it may be any of these. Among such recollections is a glimpse of the pileated's imperial brother, the ivory-billed woodpecker. It was thirty years ago. We were driving down the Frederica River, the sloop logging a good eight knots before a stiff nor'wester, about fifteen miles north of Brunswick, Georgia. Pointing to starboard, the mate exclaimed, "Look at that funny crow!"

I looked. Swinging in regulation undulating curves, not fifty feet from the sloop's bow, passed an ivory-bill, so close I could even distinguish its sex—a male. Knowing that ivorybills usually travel in pairs, I watched eagerly for his mate, but we were an eighth of a mile beyond before she followed. The ladies of the romantic nineties were cautious!

## II

The red-headed woodpecker is one of the first birds I learned to identify and, odd as it may seem, it was not the easy task it would be under normal conditions. I was about ten years old when I saw a bird with carmine head, white below, and with black wings, sweeping out from a treetop, catching insects on the wing, returning from each foray to the same perch. A flycatcher, of course, but an exhaustive study of Wilson's and Nuttall's Ornithologies, the only two bird books I possessed at the time, revealed no red-headed flycatcher. The next sight of the bird, this time on a tree trunk, cleared the puzzling situation.

In the long interval between, I have watched and admired the easy assurance, playfulness, and d'Artagnan air of this rollicking blade wearing so jauntily the colors of his country. He, like many other of our brightly-colored birds, has had to struggle against not only natural forces of destruction but the more deadly one of the slowly dying unjust prejudices clustered around the banner of "SHOOT HIM DOWN!"

Next time the opportunity offers, listen to one of the redheads' family conferences, when the brown youngsters are old enough to participate. The arguments, loud calls, uncensored remarks, and unwoodpecker-like notes would shame a democratic convention! The hearer might even imagine Dawes was addressing the Senate. Watch a pair harry a red squirrel who perhaps had broken into their cache of beechnuts. The opening attack is delivered in apparent anger, but as the mêlée progresses, gradually changes into its real character of pure teasing. The birds generally come out top dog, driving the wood-be thief into hiding and although my sympathies usually are with the under canine, in this case the flaunting flag of victory waved above the miscreant wins my unqualified approval.

I have seen a pair isolate one of the rufous-coated imps on top of a fence-post and bedevil him so persistently that he fairly frothed at the mouth, thereby releasing some of the beechnuts stowed in his pouch. These, one of the aggressors carried off and hid, the other meanwhile continuing the attack until the freebooter gave up the rest of the loot.

Most of the genus possess a limited vocabulary, but the redhead voices an astounding array of chirps, cheeps, and rough notes including a *wickup-wickup-wickup-wickup*, shorter but resembling the flicker's rolling call.

Like his relative the ant-eating woodpecker of the West, who digs holes in an old stump and fills them with acorns,—sometimes traveling miles to obtain the oak-seed,—the redhead stuffs surplus food away in crannies. He lacks the instinct to chisel holes for these stores, always stowing them in some natural cavity, but

Many an interesting game of hide-and-seek was played in the branches

the tendency toward forehandedness is there. I have frequently found large black beetles with all legs carefully removed, under crannies of bark—secreted, probably, at a time when the guardian angel of coleoptera may have been wandering off in the woods somewhere, watching the nymphs and fauns at play. The utter indifference of the stronger forms of life toward the suffering and torture of the weaker ones is not conducive of a belief that the Monitor of all cares very much whether or not they suffer.

Most members of the woodpecker family remain on the home grounds throughout the year, or migrate locally if driven to it by extreme cold or lack of food. Two exceptions are the redhead and the flicker.

An old maple stands in the meadow about six hundred feet from the house. I have watched flickers bound south through the narrow defile of our valley in late September, and it seemed every one of them lit on that isolated tree. Migrating sharp-shinned hawks always headed for it, too, and many an interesting game of hide-and-seek was played in the branches with flickers in the rôle of evader.

Down shot the little murderer! Round the limb slipped the woodpecker. Swinging in an upward arc, the pursuer hurtled back, executing a series of short-armed dives, but I 've never seen one succeed in catching the pursued one. The most persistent aggressors were the young hawks, the slate-colored elders merely making a single swoop, then shooting off and onward. If education is the capacity to apply experience, here was an example: the old birds probably had made the attempt many times in their youth, unsuccessfully, and wasted no time now on futile pursuit. It was evident the woodpeckers knew they were safe as long as they remained in the tree and dodged. Rarely one attempted escape by flight. If it did so . . . that was the end. The feathered demon had it before it was fairly clear of the leaves.

The New York Conservation Commission has established a zone from Canada to Long Island

Sound, along the eastern edge of New York State, against advancing hordes of the gypsy moth. The men who have been through this section of the Taconic Hills are fine upstanding Americans who take a personal interest and examine every tree as carefully as though it were their own. The moth usually lays the fatal egg cluster on the trunk but it may be deposited in a crevice or limb impossible to see from the ground. In the descriptive circular no mention is made of assistants, but Messrs. Downy and Hairy are on the job continually.

The downy woodpecker is such a confiding little fellow that nearly every move of his has been watched and recorded. Big Brother Hairy is rarer and comes to the suet counter only when regular food is scarce. Anything written of him is equally applicable to his lesser confrère. In a dead golden-sweet apple-tree, over an eighth of a mile west of the house, a pair of hairy woodpeckers have raised a family every year for the last six years. This tree is one of a number which formed an orchard near the original farm-house. None would guess a home had ever been there. All remnants, even the foundation, have disappeared, and the gaunt old trees are rapidly following.

Seated under a cluster of small maples, one day in early May, I watched the interesting courting antics of the pair. The jaunty male's favorite position was one in which he appeared to be almost standing on his tail. With bill upright, wings thrown forward, and tail widespread he repeated over and over what was undoubtedly intended for a love-song, a series of notes divided between chuckles and whistles. But the strangest, most mystifying performance was a series of backward drops on the under side of a limb inclined about forty-five degrees. Newton would have received here no assistance toward discovery of his famous law; indeed, the law was apparently suspended for the particular benefit of Mr. Hairy while these Houdini antics were executed. Why did n't the little acrobat fall when he released his claws? Studying his movements carefully through the binoculars, I came to the conclusion that at the instant of releasing his grip he jerked his body toward the limb with sufficient impetus to catch the bark six inches or so below.

As usual, the lady pretended indifference. Assumed reluctance was ever a potent feminine wile! Wherein she differed not at all—it will hardly do to say with other two-legged ladies, so we'll compromise on just *females*. She threw him a side glance now and then, but even that meager encouragement was sufficient to stir him to additional activity.

The couple successfully evaded the dangers of wood and field with the youngsters, although my fightin' dog may have been helpful in this, for with wild short barks she chased a weasel away from the vicinity. This bundle of energy and viciousness is the worst enemy the woodpeckers have here. They are not afraid of black-snakes, and attacked courageously whenever one was encountered. Moreover, they usually select a home tree too large for reptiles to climb.

One day in November, after the leaves had relinquished their hold on all but oak branches, I began getting down next winter's wood. A hairy lit on a dead tree near by, peering inquisitively at me around the trunk. It suddenly occurred to me the day was too warm for chopping, so I dropped the ax on top of a butt, filled the pipe, and spent the next four hours playing "follow my leader."

That fellow lit on two hundred and eighteen different trees, an average of nearly one a minute! The longest time he remained on one tree was seven minutes. This was a dead chestnut with most of the bark still adhering. By far the larger proportion of the trees were old chestnuts, and under their loosely attached covering he found most successful hunting. Rough-bark species were preferred—chestnuts, oaks, old maples and hickories, about in the order named. Smooth-barked ones received little notice. He did not alight on a single whitewood, although they were common. Birches were included occasionally, and in one of these clumps he had a short argument with a chickadee whose territory he was invading. The chickadee is small, but he has plenty of pluck and he informed Mr. Red Topknot that his society was not desired. Being a gentleman, the hairy readily acceded to the request to "move on."

If this average held good, it meant he inspected something like five hundred and fifty trees in a ten-hour working-day; a conservative estimate, for during spring and summer his time-card would show a much longer day!

His capacity for locating a grub was not always accurate. Many borings I examined entered the burrow above the grub, but near enough so the extensive barbed tongue could gather in the dainty. Very rarely the first attempt would miss the mark entirely, starting below or at one side. Sometimes the mistake was discovered coincident with the removal of the first few chips: at others, the false hole was driven quite deeply before correction. Just how the birds locate these hidden delicacies is uncertain. Naturally the first conclusion is that the sense of hearing is the primary factor. This is probably correct, although some of the curled ugly specimens I have brought to light on January days looked and acted too frozen for even the slightest movement.

Young smooth-barked hickories honeycombed within half an inch of the surface by borers which entered from the ground were not drilled by the woodpeckers. Many of these internally riddled trees were cut down in the nest vicinity and the birds either had not known they held food or had considered the effort necessary to penetrate the tough wood too onerous.

Their attachment to the home location was remarkable and unique among birds of this vicinity. I doubt if they ever ventured more than a mile from this remnant of an orchard. North of these old trees an oblong open field was convenient for felling next year's wood-supply. On my trips up there one of the pair never failed to be near by. Several times the

The jaunty male's favorite position was one in which he appeared to be almost standing on his tail

male's curiosity conquered his aloofness and he ventured within thirty feet, answering each ax blow with his sharp *queek* for minutes at a time. Maybe he thought I was some strange kind of woodpecker, intruding upon his premises, and that swinging ax a novel form of bill! I recall very few times, no matter what the season, that I did not see or hear a woodpecker somewhere in the vicinity. Their fondness for drumming on a hollow limb is not confined to the spring months.

While writing this, on a rather mild day in the latter part of December, I was called outside to identify a series of singular bell-like notes. They were made by Hairy's smaller brother, Downy, who had discovered a sounding-board with a peculiar resonance, producing a metallic scale similar to that of the tree-toad but higher.

Members of this genus have been accused of many crimes, from eating corn to murdering the young of other species, and with a persistency reminiscent of the dark-ages these erroneous beliefs continue to revive. As a family the woodpeckers are among man's most valuable allies in keeping insect enemies in subjection. So-called facts must always be qualified by the grade of intellect presenting them. Running down unfriendly criticisms of these birds to their source will usually reveal their bases rest on poor observation or biased judgment. Consideration for all forms of wild life is gradually extending toward the high plane it eventually will obtain in man's evolution.

Do you live here all winter alone?" is a frequent query.

"I live here the year 'round, but not *alone.* My side partner attends to household affairs and Mr. and Mrs. Sciurus usually occupy the north wing."

"Mr. and Mrs. *Who?*"

"Sciurus."

"What an odd name!"

"It fits the parties. They 're not only curious but as full of all-around impudence as anything I know. There 's one of them now."

"Oh! you mean squirrels?"

"Yes, just plain Reds. Now watch this fellow."

Down the maple trunk he came, with spasmodic jumps, and jumping down a perpendicular tree is not the simple matter it appears.

Try it and see! On he came until within five feet of our heads, scolding in moderate tempo, neck at right angles and tail jerking as though to add emphasis to his remonstrances.

Some nature writers whose imagination is limitless could interpret his language, but not possessing their ability I shall have to be content with a blanket translation to the effect that he wanted to know what all this hubbub was about under his own private tree, and would we "get-to-Kent out of there"! One could be in no doubt as to the tenor of his remarks, even if only slightly acquainted with the saucy rascal.

"Has n't he wonderful eyes!"

"Yes, but his physical prowess is more remarkable. Watch him when he finishes his speech."

After a short interval we were accepted as part of the scenery and Chatterbox ascended the maple, ran along a horizontal limb, jumped to Apple Avenue, traversed this short thoroughfare and in a few seconds reached Hickory Lane, then scampered up into the leafy haven until he found three nuts in a cluster, bit them off, and started down.

His storehouse was in an old apple-tree some distance away and the trail he always followed was a devious one, including the descent of a dead cherry-tree near his home cache.

Transporting three hickory-nuts, encased in their heavy husks, along this aërial highway is no slight engineering problem, so I slipped up behind the cherry-tree to watch the manœuvers. In a few moments he landed on the tree's opposite side and was within two feet of my head before he discovered me. What a blowing up there was! Billy Sunday's wildest denunciations would have seemed lullabies in a debate with this sputtering Vesuvius. Not alone at *my* head were invectives directed but at unnumbered ancestors. Even justifiable anger exacts a price—in this case, three nuts which fell into my hands as he let them go. The loss was only temporary, however, for on a later trip he recovered them from a crotch where I had placed them.

These little rufous-coated bundles of energy have given my mechanical bent many an interesting hour. The strength displayed in handling such a burden was amazing, but when walnuts are ripe *Hudsonicus* becomes a regular Ajax. A husky Red weighs about fifteen ounces and an unshelled walnut . . . let me see . . . I 'll go and get one and find out. . . . The scales say three ounces. The tree is about twenty-five yards north and the storehouse is under a hemlock two hundred and thirty feet away. Suppose you had to carry in your teeth a hundred or more pumpkins weighing thirty pounds apiece, on the run, a couple of miles a day, how many do you think you 'd transfer? I suspect the numeral one would be the answer, with a set of artificial molars required afterward, or perhaps a single round O would come nearer the truth.

Some years ago I was driving a horse—yes,

*horse*, not car—along the Kent road. A red squirrel came down from a butternut tree to the rail fence and started along it with a nut in his jaws. We were going at a jog and that fellow kept ahead of us on his zigzag path for half a mile and then disappeared into a tree cavity. I pulled up alongside the road and waited. Soon he reappeared and headed back for the supply station. It was a warm October day and there was nothing on my mind, so I lit the old pipe—remarks from the first mate anent its aroma, when I light up o' nights, prove its ancient lineage—and timed that round trip. In nine minutes he was back. The next journey was made in nine and one half minutes, a more dependable schedule than some of the trains on our road can boast.

A valley friend drove by, returning from delivering milk at the station.

"Hello, Rex, what 're yer doin' here all by yourself?"

"Timing a red squirrel's trips between supply and storehouse."

"Well, that all you got ter do? . . . Geddap!"

I suppose it did seem like a waste of time to that eighteen-hour-a-day dairyman. But you never can tell. Since he has seen some printed words of mine his opinion has changed. A little ink and type work marvelous transformations in the minds of many. A nonentity, maybe, up to the moment these Aladdin marks appear upon a white page, and then,—behold! an interesting member of the community.

Although red squirrels are physically perfect, the mental processes of individuals do not always react successfully to sudden emergencies. Their knack of landing on their feet when falling is extraordinary. My fighting dog occasionally scares one, probably a youngster, into relinquishing his safe perch aloft for the ground—a leap of perhaps fifteen or more feet. The little creature invariably hits the earth head up and ready to run. Pal has not caught one yet and I hope she never will, although I have n't much fear that she would get the better of it,

When walnuts are ripe Hudsonicus becomes a regular Ajax

for squirrels' teeth are sharp. Pal will tackle a woodchuck without hesitation, but is more cautious with the smaller animals.

A friend of mine was driving his car along a cement road when a red squirrel landed just ahead, on its back. A piece of dead branch was tightly gripped with all claws. Now, Red's natural tendency was to believe he was safe as long as he had his feet on a limb, and when this broke his instinct did not react quickly enough to allow him to release his hold and turn in the air so as to land right side up.

However, some members of the red-squirrel family *do* think things out. Our grape-arbor posts are of cedar and although they have been in the ground nearly ten years, some bark still remains. A few mornings ago a Red was attempting to remove a long sliver of this bark. All his strenuous jerks were futile; one end refused to part from a nailed cross-lath. His chattering brought the Real Boss to the scene. She tailed on like a sailor, helping hoist the main topsail yard (I say "she" advisedly, for sex, aside from mannerisms, is a matter of conjecture) but even the combined yanking failed to tear the fiber loose. That efficiency expert wasted no time. Down she went to the base and bit it off. After a few comments on her mate's stupidity in not doing this at first, she helped him roll the booty into two compact balls so stray ends would not trip them, and lugged it off for nest lining.

While I was clearing the weeds out of a small strawberry patch perched atop the east wall which was built to level up the space on that side of the house, a Red came bouncing along with a hickory-nut. About fifteen feet away he stopped, looked me over suspiciously, decided the passage was n't safe, and hid the nut under a rock. Then he advanced cautiously, stood on his hind legs, whisked his tail several times, and finally decided I was n't dangerous. Back he went to the hidden treasure, retrieved it, and raced past.

The only flaw in a perfect argument for reason against instinct was that he stowed the food away while I watched him. The squirrel family's forehandedness in laying up the winter food supply results in storing away more than they can use where provender is plentiful. I have found fifteen quarts of shelled hickory-nuts in one cache. Little of this horde goes to waste, however, for others, less energetic, steal the stuff. Blue jays and woodpeckers make off with beech-nuts and chestnuts, and once I watched a chipmunk take hickory-nuts as fast as a Red deposited them in an old apple-tree hollow. The striped imp waited until the provider was out of sight before making his foray. The hole was shallow and held thirty or forty nuts, and the thief seemed to take away only those which were added.

Did the chipmunk leave the others for nest eggs? Here 's a little point for the super-naturalist! A thing he did do was to miscalculate the time of one of Red's visits and they met at the entrance. There was no doubt whatever about Red's understanding what Stripes was up to. A wild chase ensued, ending with the disappearance of Munk into his burrow.

Old Dame Nature is usually particular in demanding obedience to her rules, but sometimes she nods. The law of survival of the fittest may be shelved: the strong help the weak even unwittingly, as proved in the case of Stripes. But the weak, as represented by our red-furred friend in an encounter with the strong, as personified by the writer, are not necessarily backward in administration of a scolding. . . .

The chicken house has been tenantless for two years. I took it over occasionally to see that no ghaisties, ghosts, or leprechauns have made it their abode. One early summer day I pulled out a nest box and found it occupied by a red squirrel's small family. Mother was extremely reluctant to leave, and called shrilly for assistance. This arrived quickly along a limb just outside the open front of the house. She joined her rescuer and I became the target of their combined remonstrances. Each raucous comment by Father was followed with two thin *cheeps* from Mother, who never failed to keep time with his lead, vary as he would. They kept it up for half an hour, seeming to be affected by that particular form of egotism possessed by those who love the sound of their own voices.

Watching the red squirrels, I have often wished that the intense energy of these restless, quick-moving little fellows could be transformed into useful production. It would perform no small percentage of the world's work.

Among their little-known accomplishments is long-distance swimming. One was taken aboard a canoe from a Maine lake after swimming one half mile: it did not appear to be tired and undoubtedly would have made the near-by shore unassisted. In ratio to weight this would mean that a hundred-and-fifty pound athlete who possessed relative endurance could swim seventy-five miles continuously. Aspirants for English-Channel marine honors please note!

Though there are eighteen shellbark hickory-trees on this quarter-square mile, only three of them bear seed: two which stand fifty feet from our porch, and one fine old patriarch a couple of hundred feet to the northwest. The others are on such thin soil that they have all they can do to exist and lack the surplus strength necessary to produce nuts. Consequently these three trees receive assiduous attention during daylight hours from Reds and Grays, and by night from moon-eyed flying squirrels.

The line of approach to the two yard trees was along an apple highway. Last autumn I widened the jump to about seven feet. Both species made it easily. Wire guards were put around the hickories and more apple-tree limbs severed until the only way to get at the nuts was to make an almost horizontal jump of twelve feet. These interferences did not prevent the Grays from making their objective. That leap of a dozen feet was a thrilling exhibition of parabolic grace. If I possessed the same relative muscular strength, I could make the brook—over eight hundred feet away—in one hop.

Though foiled at first, the Reds soon evolved a successful plan of approach. This necessitated an entire change in their tactics and compelled them to start the attack at the base of a maple which stands within a few feet of the porch steps. It is odd that an animal with sense enough to figure out a complicated transportation problem of this sort, did not refrain from biting off nuts before they ripened. A plain case of appetite overruling the hoarding instinct.

I have often seen red-tailed hawks attempt to capture gray squirrels in tree-tops, but have seldom witnessed a successful culmination of their efforts. Once when I chanced to be well hidden in brush the pursued acted as though he thought the hawk were playing some kind of game. He would slide around the limb and poke his head out sideways. "Never tagged me; try again, old scout!"

In early spring when sap begins its upward flow, both kinds of squirrels will gouge out hollows—usually in maples, more rarely in birch limbs—and drink the juice which collects there. While not exactly intoxicating, and outside Mr. Volstead's jurisdiction, the liquid certainly produces a somnolent effect and the squirrels are most frequently captured by aërial prowlers when under its influence.

> Drink lightly from this maple bowl,
> Lest hawks lug off thy furry soul!

Two such tragedies, which I witnessed, happened in the month of April. I wonder what business old Bacchus had wandering about at that time of year. I have often approached an imbiber by slow moves and once actually touched some gray fur before it woke up.

Most of us have at some time dreamed of falling from a tree. Of course our dream is a hereditary transference from the days when man was arboreal: it may be that one of our enemies in those far-gone centuries was some form of flying monster and we released our hold for the same reason that a certain squirrel did which I observed last autumn. I was enjoy-

His method of escape was simple: he let go all holds

ing an afternoon pipe in the hammock, watching lazy October cumuli drift across the western blue, when I saw a Gray gathering seeds from the top of a tall maple about two hundred feet up the hill. A dark spot appeared over the ridge and slanted for the little forager. His method of escape was as simple as our dream: he let go all holds and disappeared in the underbrush! The onrushing pirate rose in a long sweeping arc, passed overhead, and I recognized one of our rare birds of prey, a dark form of the rough-legged hawk.

John Burroughs was at a loss to understand how the squirrels invariably cut through the thin side of a butternut closest to the meat. The reason they could always do this seems perfectly obvious to me—a sense of smell which in these animals is extremely acute. I collected some nuts and put them into a box in the workshop, thinking they were safe enough there. Not so! A squirrel went in through the open door, climbed up on the table, and carried off fully a quarter of the contents before I caught him at it. Then the box was covered but the door left open purposely. Next morning there was a hole in the corner of the container and nearly half the provender had disappeared.

It is this same olfactory keenness which enables the squirrel to locate a nut or an acorn buried the previous autumn and retrieve it by digging through a foot of snow. As far as I have observed, this accomplishment is confined mainly to the Grays, for they hibernate less than their rufous confrères and are likely to roam abroad during any fine winter day.

There is a belief current in the country-side that the Gray is harried and driven off favorable feeding grounds by the Red. In the abstract there is a certain amount of truth in the notion, for the smaller animal does possess a more aggressive personality and in an argument generally carries the day by sheer bluff, for in all the encounters I have witnessed I have never seen any bloodshed. The fights are staged and followed through with loud battle-cries and a continuous series of lightning-like retreats and offensives. Sometimes the antagonists become so engrossed in the argument that they appear to lose sight of everything save each other, and I have had them scamper across my feet apparently without realizing that my underpinning was movable.

Though not exactly a Cid in courage, the Gray is by no means lacking in this virtue, especially when the youngsters are in jeopardy. I have a scar on the first finger of my right hand where a gray squirrel bit to the bone when I incautiously reached into what I thought was a crow's nest. She bit and held on. I dragged the furry fury out clinging with teeth and claws, and shook her off. She caught on a limb a few feet below and came back, but fortunately not for me! The jar had evidently changed the current of her thoughts. Into the nest she went, and out she came with a tiny ball in her mouth. She seemed uncertain for a moment what to do, but suddenly remembered a near-by hole and scampered over a waving limb to the refuge while I scuttled to the ground.

There is no doubt whatever which one of us was the more thoroughly scared. She transferred her other three infants and stuck her head out of the hole. While not exactly making a face at me, she indicated quite plainly that she dared me to come on.

There is an old Grayback tending hereabout who has no respect at all for Reds, Pal, or me! When he is at work aloft, all others keep off and he sees to it that they do. If an intruder starts to ascend the tree he will carefully lay in a crotch the nut he is working on and meet the advancing party more than half-way. What he does and says, goes!

In earlier days I spent much time among the fishermen of Maine and with the insouciance of youth was seriously considering entering their profession of hauling the cod and haddock of Georges and Newfoundland Banks into a dory, for a livelihood. I drifted into another current, but contact with that strenuous life convinced me Conscience and Remorse had been sunk without trace, with large grate-bar anchors firmly attached. These two bugaboos would never trouble me again.

An illusion! A certain sense of sportsmanship retired the shotgun as unfair, but I still clung to a twenty-two caliber rifle, and constant practice made this a deadly weapon at my shoulder. Targets were mainly old cans, bottles, et cetera, but in an evil moment I drew on a gray squirrel and wounded him. There is no satisfactory explanation of why some mental pictures endure more poignantly than others: they just *do*, and that poor animal proved my vauntedly extinct remorse was as much alive as ever. It happened many years ago, but as I write this all the sharpness of that memory revives and the recollection is anything but a pleasant one. The little gray victim with his coppery back was a martyr, though, who really accomplished reform. I made a gentleman's agreement with myself as he lay dead at my feet: NEVER AGAIN! And that promise was not merely "a scrap of paper."

## WHISKASHON

ISOLATING two men in a cabin may be tantamount to manslaughter, as O. Henry remarked, and again it may not be. Jo and I spent a winter in an abandoned lumber camp near Moosehead Lake without getting into a fight; in fact, we parted in the spring like ideal honeymooners, without having had even an argument! And, what 's more, I know several men with whom I 'd risk the same experiment to-day. I 'm not going to name them, for fear they 'd take me up on it.

Such close contact reveals a man's inner nature as nothing else can, and one trait of Jo's stood out prominently. He was truthful. Many of the incidents in the following story and that entitled "Ghost of the Graylands" I extracted from him by main strength, for he was not given to talking—in which particular he was true to type, being a descendant of those taciturn French voyageurs who conquered the Northern wilderness.

When I told of seeing a snowy owl catch a trout he was reminded of the first part of his story, and gradually we wove out of our experiences "Whiskashon" and "Ghost of the Graylands."

The factor, MacLaren, was Scotch, therefore truthful, accurate, and a keen naturalist. Old Dr. Johnson might not agree with me, judging from his definition of "oats"—"food for mules and Scotch"!

The luminous wonder of northern lights blotted out the stars except in a small area to the south'ard, the sky a sea of soft crimson fading through many shades of pink into a space of elusive purple above the back trail. Then suddenly all warm tints were gone; cold greens and yellows filled the heavens. Great fingers of shimmering light rayed upward, quivering with prismatic colors as they faded and reappeared. By many a camp-fire Jo had watched the aurora pageantry before drifting to sleep, but now the gods were running wild, spreading every hue riotously across the broad canvas of infinity. Enthralled, he lay in his blanket while the glowing bands shot in league-long waves far beyond the zenith.

"*Some* show! The mail has got to go on, though." Tumbling out of his warm spruce-bough-lined nest in the snow, Jo raked the camp-fire coals together and threw on fresh wood. As he took coffee-pot and spider from his sled, his glance fell on two tiny points of fire in a near-by evergreen.

"Never miss a trick, do you? Who asked you to join this outfit, anyway? Suppose you 're going all the way to the post? Well, old-timer, we 'll make it to-day all right if wind and snow hold off."

The four huskies squatted in a semicircle while he made coffee. The leader, a magnificent animal, raised a paw against his coat.

"Want your breakfast, eh?" Jo gave them

each a large frozen fish. Instead of wolfing down the food as do members of most teams, with intent of getting it out of sight, then stealing from others, they quietly gnawed away with half-closed eyes, in undisturbed content.

Jo had owned them for two years and, believing it possible to control dogs without whip or club, had trained them by methods of his own.

"Can't be done!" said other drivers. "A wolf's a wolf, and the only way you can make him mind is with a club."

"They're not *all* wolf. I 'm going to get at the dog in them. It can be done and I 'm going to do it."

The first half-year was a long, tough fight, but Jo possessed patience, and slowly it dawned on the animals that he had determination also. During the first part of their re-education forcible means sometimes were necessary, but he used a switch, not a club. Breaking them of stealing one another's rations was accomplished by the simple expedient of giving them enough food. In the North, life needs plenty of fuel to keep out the bitter cold, and very few living things, especially dogs, receive sufficient. Jo gave his team two good meals a day, either buying from Indians or catching extra fish himself. Near-starvation had made them three quarter savage, and it was many months before they were semi-tamed. Persistence accomplished the task, and now they took their positions between the traces quietly, ready and eager to go.

Meanwhile the feathered pigmy in the tree had been watching every move of Jo's breakfast preparations.

"Suppose you 've got to have yours, too. Come and get it!" said Jo, holding out a piece of bacon. Unhesitatingly the jay lit on his finger, grabbed the titbit, and started eating.

"Here, I 've got work to do!" Jo said, shaking him off. "Beat it back to your perch!"

When the dogs were harnessed, Whiskashon lit on the sled, selected a crevice between packs, and settled comfortably into it.

"Where 's your ticket? Who gave you permission to ride on this train?" The jay cocked its head, looked up with sharp black eyes, shook his feathers, and merely readjusted its position. "Foxy enough to wait until the dogs were buckled in, were n't you? Well, I guess that 's ticket enough, but it 's got to be punched."

Reaching down, Jo caught the bird. It made little protest, even when held against a convenient tree and the end of its tail neatly cleft into a V with the ax.

"There, now, I 'll know you. Get back into your seat and let 's go!"

A crust over the deep snow, strong enough to hold a man and under two inches of fresh-fallen flakes, made traveling conditions perfect. Ahead stretched the wide river road flanked by walls of spruces, reflecting dimly the mutable Aurora still flickering. "Mush on, old scouts! If a blizzard does n't hit in, we 'll be home by three o'clock."

Into the fading prismatic path they went at an easy jog, the shrewd leader knowing better than to set a fast pace at the beginning of a day's run. Jo was behind at the pole. No need of breaking trail with snow-shoes; in fact, they had been lashed on the sled every day this trip. He just tagged along easily, calling words of encouragement to the willing dogs swinging onward with their brushy tails as erect as totem poles.

When the still dawn dissipated the pageant ahead, "Nicktail" came out of his nook, shook himself, eyed Jo, and flew off into the bordering trees.

"So, that 's the game! Afraid to travel in the dark! Now it 's light, shake me cold!"

Jo was wrong: the bird was out for exercise, keeping a little in advance of the sled, scolding raucously now and then at other jays who attempted to "cut in" or sending a flock of crossbills scurrying in all directions as he dived among them with a shriek.

Toward noon the team was headed into a small grove and unharnessed. A little work with the belt-ax, and a small fire crackled.

Nicktail flew down and attempted to seize a mouthful

Water was boiling quickly and before adding coffee Jo used some to mix up a batch of pancake batter, having tempered it with a little snow. When cooked on one side, the flapjack was tossed, and just as it descended into the pan, Nicktail flew down, lit on the edge of the skillet, and attempted to seize a mouthful. When the heat hit through his cold feet he went up in the air like a climbing black-duck.

"Well, you damphul! Maybe you'll wait next time. I've a good mind to let you go hungry for tryin' such a trick! Here, take this!" and Jo tossed a bit of the cake toward the bird. It never touched the snow but was neatly caught in mid-air and lugged to a near-by branch.

In the stern code of the North one lesson is learned quickly by all: food when found must be devoured at once or it may be seized by a lurking enemy. In this instance fear of loss was not without foundation: Nicktail was rapidly gulping down pieces as large as he could manage. The job was almost finished when three gray forms shot in and dived directly at him. The last bit—an extra-large chunk—became wedged crossways in his bill. He struggled desperately to swallow, but one of the jay robbers seized it and downed the morsel without effort. Food! There was more below. Down they swooped—two into the pan and one on Jo's shoulder.

"Gwan out of this, you nervy divvils!" exclaimed Jo, sweeping them aside. "Stay off there till I 'm ready to give you what 's comin' to you, if any!"

They stood in the snow within a few feet until he tossed them the last piece. As long as the trio saw more cake in Jo's hand they remained close by, but when the final remnant was passed out the recipient started for the woods with the other two in full cry. They realized that dinner was over. In the words of P. Henry (with the omission of one letter): "If that be reason—make the most of it!"

"I guess I 'd better light out of here or they 'll come back and eat one of my dogs!"

The jays' cries ceased, then were renewed with wild accentuation.

"Found something! Guess I 'll slip in and see."

The animated discussion centered around a horizontal spruce limb. In the dim light Jo could not make out the cause of their remarks. When his eye-focus adjusted to the gloom he saw a marten stretched flat on a branch, motionless. While he watched, one of the birds ventured too close. A swift paw-flick caught the aggressor across the back, pulled it to the marten's chest. A single snap . . . and for that brown-coated animal dinner was served!

"Maybe that 'll teach the rest of you to leave a bit of chained lightning like that fellow, alone! I dunno. Sometimes you 've got sense enough, others just plain dumb. Anyway, he did n't get you, Nicktail. Come on if you 're goin' the rest of the way! We 've got to vamoose."

About three o'clock they dashed into the post enclosure, heads and tails aloft, with all the flourish of a tally-ho.

"Where did you pick up your friend?" asked MacLaren, the factor, after greetings were over. He indicated Nicktail perched atop the sled baggage.

"Joined the procession this morning. Had to carry him as a passenger until it was light. He traveled under his own power the rest of the way."

"You mean he let you transport him on the sled?"

"Just that! Stowed himself away among the sacks and hung on like a weasel to a rabbit."

"That certainly is interesting! We'll keep an eye on him."

A rubbish heap at the edge of the woods was a favorite hunting ground for jays that had congregated around the post for winter. The dogs, being well nourished and housed, did not bother rummaging among the debris. Excepting a few nocturnal prowlers, the birds had a monopoly. One day Jo saw Nicktail break open a pasteboard box containing beads, which had been thrown away inadvertently. Seizing a bead, he flew to a limb, grasped his find firmly with the toes of both feet, threw back his head, and hit the bead with his bill, putting into the stroke all the strength of his neck muscles. In rapid succession the shots were delivered so accurately that his toes were not struck.

"If I could teach you to handle an ax, you 'd be *some* lumber-jack! *I* would n't swing a pick with that speed at anything between *my* feet!—I'd lose a toe or two, sure! Now I wonder if you 're goin' to advertise your find as the other chumps do?"

Discovering it was not food, and that it was unbreakable, Nicktail grabbed half a dozen of the glass globules and started hiding the treasures under crevices of bark. He worked in silence, swiftly and furtively. The box was n't half empty before the band discovered what was up. Willing and enthusiastic assistance completed the job speedily.

"Their sense of location," said the factor, "is remarkably keen. In the fall, when they begin to gather round the post, I often cut salt pork into pieces and throw a handful into the brush and grass. Very seldom do they fail to find every piece, sometimes more than a dozen in number. Many of the bits, of course, are in plain sight but others completely hidden are found also. Their sense of smell does not aid them greatly, as we can prove easily. There are none in sight now, so we 'll cover this piece of fish with a rag and see if they can find it."

In a little while three birds appeared, one walking directly over the hidden food.

"Now, if we show it 's here," said the factor, raising the cloth, "we 'll get action."

They certainly did: he had scarcely lifted the covering before those three impetuous free-booters fell upon the fish—a squalling, fighting trio, dragging the prize off and away.

Nicktail became very tame. Jo attempted, unsuccessfully, to lure him into the main room. The sky was the only roof he had ever known; a darker canopy made him suspicious. He clung to his roost in the dense evergreens, but was always on deck when Jo appeared, flying to greet him with rough notes of welcome and usually alighting on his head or shoulder. When the bird perched on his finger Jo marveled at his lightness.

"You ain't any heavier than a robin, but look twice as big. Suppose it 's that coat you 've got on!"

Jo was right: the feathers were of a curiously rough texture, each barb separated, not locked by hundreds of tiny hooks as are some feathers. This was especially true of the underneath plumage. It was a wonderful air-trap, keeping body warmth in and cold out. As cold increased, his feathers fluffed gradually until at twenty or thirty degrees below zero Nicktail seemed an animated ball.

Daylight hours were short and Jo spent most of them tramping, adding many an interesting side-light to his knowledge of wild life. He had occasionally found excavations around mouse snow-tunnels which puzzled him. Absence of footprints proved they were not made by animals. The mystery was cleared one day when Jo began digging with his mittens at a fresh mouse-hole. Nicktail hopped in and added his bit by helping kick out the snow with his feet.

"Well! now I know who was after those mice! Probably only tried to dig one out when you saw it dive in. Regular little husky for diggin', ain't you?"

Nicktail was an interested, tireless companion, and Jo always investigated side trips when the bird uttered calls of surprise. There was a distinct difference in the timbre of various cries and Jo seldom made a mistake in correctly interpreting their significance.

His loud alarm cries, one afternoon, led Jo to a cow moose helpless in the snow. She had floundered out of the beaten yard-path and struggling had so weakened her she was unable to return. With a snow-shoe he cleared a course to the runway, dug the stranded animal free, slapped her on the back, and started her into the haven.

"We 'll keep this dark. If the Indians ever discover moose so close to the post, they 'll clean 'em out in no time."

This compact with himself and Nicktail was kept even to the extent of not telling the factor. Jo trusted MacLaren, but there just was no need of saying a thing about it.

On another occasion Jo saw Nicktail peering into what seemed to be an old nest, about fifteen feet up a small spruce. Closer observation revealed a bill sticking over the edge. Although this was early in March, temperatures well below zero were the rule and it did not occur to Jo that any birds *could* raise a family under such frigid conditions. The right-angled limbs, spaced at convenient intervals, made ascent of the tree easy and Jo's hand was almost on the mother bird's back before she flew off. Another Whiskashon!

Looking down into the nest, he saw nothing but rabbit's fur and feathers. Slipping off a mitten, he pushed a finger down and found, under this warm coverlet, four eggs. Jo realized that if the mother remained away even for a short time the eggs might freeze, although embedded in a wonderfully snug cache, so he descended at once and had not reached the foot of the tree before the parent returned and settled down.

"Well, you certainly are the original 'early bird,' to start your domestic operations with three feet of snow below you!"

"I 'm hitting the trail to-morrow, Mac, and what to do with this bird I dunno. He 's company, all right, but he 's trouble, too. Besides, he would n't stick for two hundred miles: he 'd get down into that strange country and maybe lose himself. I 'll grab him in the morning and you keep him locked up for a few days."

This program was followed and Jo swung off on his southern route. When he returned, late one evening nearly two months afterward, his first query was: "How 's old Nicktail?"

"I let him out two days after you left," MacLaren replied. "He would n't have lived another twenty-four hours indoors, and he tried his best to bust the window-panes, at that. He disappeared, and I did n't see him for weeks, but he 's been round occasionally lately. Maybe you 'll see him in the morning."

"Chatterin' jays! how you do run on, Mac!"

There was a hint—merely a touch—of far-off spring in the late April sun as Jo lit his pipe and stepped out next morning. The first live thing he saw was Nicktail, atop a picket of the notch stockade, with four well-fledged dark grayish-brown youngsters decorating pickets.

"Well, I 'll be shot! I never guessed you were *that* kind of a bird!"

# GHOST OF THE GRAYLANDS

"WELL, what 'll I do now?—dump these mail-bags on the 'boggan or shoulder 'em? Some mess!" grunted Joe as he stepped out of the canoe, gave his cramped knees a shake to ease their stiffness, his body one likewise to throw off the damp snow clinging an inch thick on his clothes. He hauled the birch-bark up on a tiny semicircle of beach, turned it over, throwing out the heavy cargo of white flakes.

"I guess it 'll be easier draggin' the stuff. Firstly, I 'll grease her up."

The toboggan was taken from its cache, a piece of bacon rind rubbed over the smooth bottom, mail-sacks and other duffel arranged and firmly tied; then a drag on the old pipe and a short rest before starting the final lap on the two-hundred-mile route. It was after eight o'clock, but daylight still lingered; twi-

An old Wapacuthu struck Jo's head a terrific blow

lights are long and pleasant in the North country.

"Don't have to worry about settin' these woods on fire," Jo remarked as he emptied his pipe. "One good thing I 'll say for this storm, though: it knocks skeeters and black-flies. That 's a heap big help, too," he added, looking at his red-blotched hands.

Leaving the shelter of spruces, he bent his head to the moaning wind and started across the open barren. Jo knew that trail, could have followed it under any conditions except blizzards. He was half-way, pulling hard on the reluctant 'boggan, leaning well forward.

"This is spring, eh? Month of May!" His contemptuous growls were cut short by a terrific blow on the head. He turned his neck, glimpsing for an instant a great feathered form which sheered off and disappeared in the blinding snow.

"An old Wapacuthu! I 've never known one of 'em to have spunk enough for that." He touched a cold streak on his cheek. "Damned if he didn't draw blood right through this fur cap! Now . . . . I wonder . . . So *that's* it!" His eyes rested on four eggs almost at his feet.

Jo waited a few moments, thinking the bird might return. It did not, so he swerved to one side and went on.

"Maybe she mistook my cap for some kind of an animal and let go before she knew it was me: probably scared some, too, or she 'd come back. Well, old girl, I *am* comin' back and kind o' keep watch of you and your family planted 'way out here in this open spot!"

Half an hour later Jo entered the post's fenced inclosure and clasped MacLaren's hand in undemonstrative Northern greeting.

"Been looking for you last three hours," said the factor. "Your supper 's on the table. Eat first, talk afterwards." A long speech for the factor.

While Jo was satisfying his hunger in a more dexterous than delicate manner, the factor was sorting the mail, which was all for members of the post. Pipes were lit, rough chairs drawn before the fireplace, and the two men conversed with that restrained use of words bred in all who live in the silent places. Having most information to impart, Jo did the talking while the factor listened. It was one of two dissipations he indulged in yearly. The other was the coming of Indians with the winter's catch of furs to be traded in for supplies.

"Suppose the Ojibways have n't come down yet? Too thick to see if their tepees were outside when I got here."

"No, not yet. Excepting this throw-back it 's been an early spring and I 'm expecting them 'most any day now."

The factor had noticed the scratch on Jo's forehead when he removed his cap, but made no comment or inquiry. Curiosity exists, but it is sternly suppressed among men of the North; it is part of wisdom, frequently, *not* to know.

"An old Wapacuthu struck me about two

miles back. Almost walked on to her nest."

"Never knew one to go after a man," said the factor.

"Neither did I. My head was down low: I guess she mistook the old mink cap for an animal."

"That 's very likely. We 'll go look her over. The birds are not rare, but their nests are seldom found."

Sometime during the short night the snow-storm ceased, the early dawn breaking clear and warm.

"How about tramping a bit this morning, Mac? The breeze is strong enough to hold off the flies."

"All right!"

The factor called his assistant, telling him to watch the north end of the lake and fire a gun if the Indians appeared. Failure to meet them would give the H. B. C. a black mark which it would take many years to erase, and the rival French post across the lake would greatly benefit by such a blunder.

The bright sun and a strong southwest breeze were rapidly dissipating the damp snow. As they walked through the tundra longspurs soared above with tingling song.

"Man! but they make me homesick!" exclaimed MacLaren, watching their spiral flights as they flooded surrounding space with melody.

"Are n't there two kinds?" queried the matter-of-fact Jo.

"Yes, that 's the chestnut-collared longspur with the black breast and brown band on the back of his neck. This one with dark head and throat, dropping toward us like a large butterfly, is the Lapland longspur."

MacLaren's comparison was apt: with wings held at an acute angle upward, down the lark came in long parachute descent, reaching earth in a short slanting flight.

Male ptarmigans, their winter dress of white variegated with beautiful brown, mounted little hillocks, giving their peculiar hoarse chuckling call. After the long winter, life was bubbling over, intent upon crowding all possible pleasure into the summer days.

Reaching the nest, Jo and MacLaren found the mother absent; nor did she return while they remained. Another egg had been added.

"Looks to me as though some of the eggs were a good deal older than others."

"Keen eye, Jo! They are laid at long intervals. "You 'll probably find one or two hatched if you come back in a few days. See anything else peculiar?"

"Why, one of them is ridged lengthwise!"

"That 's it! The snowy owl is the only bird I know who lays eggs like that."

Three days later a fleet of four canoes debouched into the lake from the river a mile north. MacLaren trained glasses on the white specks.

"Not the chief! Part of his tribe from the western section."

In irregular formation they came on. As each landed the factor held out his hand. There was no word of greeting, only a steady, long hand-clasp. Tents or tepees were at once pitched and crackling camp-fires gleamed brighter as the long dusk deepened.

A flotilla of five arrived next morning. One of these Indians said to the factor:

"Chief, him come. One sun."

How did he, who had spent the winter fifty miles east of his chief's camping ground, know?

The setting sun was only a short distance above the far shore, but its oblique course would keep it in the sky for an hour when the chief and his retinue came into sight, strung out into single file, the distance between canoes maintained with military exactness.

Among Southern Indians tribal customs are waning or have vanished. Not so here in the North! This chief stood in the bow of his canoe, silhouetted against the western sky—haughty, regal, a king!—while his squaw drove the craft shoreward, with deft strong strokes.

Factor and chief gripped hands: sharp

beady black eyes looked long and intently into gray. Turning to each of his tribe ashore the chief gave the same steady look and solemn hand-clasp. Not a spoken word.

This ceremony over, the chief waved his hand to the floating canoes, and not until that permission was given did they approach land. From each birch-bark carefully wrapped bundles of precious furs were brought and stacked in front of the chief's tent to be exchanged next day for trinkets and necessities. One would think that after enduring the hardships of an Arctic winter in gathering these treasures, the trappers would be anxious to know their worth, in barter. If they felt that way, they gave no indication of it. The morning was well advanced before the chief carried his pack into the post.

In the old days little sticks were given in varying numbers corresponding to each skin's value, and as many subtracted from the total as the numbers marked on the articles selected by the Indians until he had obtained

Scarcely pausing in his flight, he extended one leg and hooked a fine trout

all the goods his sticks would buy. Nowadays the Indians trust the factor's word; although the chief understood little English, he watched every motion of the factor and his assistant as they appraised each skin. This transaction was business reduced to its simplest form. The factor valued the pelts, his assistant entering the amount under the owner's name. By nightfall the work was done. With a snap, Henry closed the large account-book, the skins were stored in the loft, and the most important day of the year at the post was over.

"Jo, how about letting me take your place this trip back? It 's over a year since I 've been outside and I 'm getting stale."

"Suits me. Ask MacLaren."

The factor acquiesced readily. Henry left next evening, preferring to travel mostly at night because then insects were less annoying. He went out light, the mail stowed away inside his pack, and Jo took up his duties as assistant.

Mother Snowy was at home on the next visit

and so reluctant to leave that Jo almost stepped on her before she arose. This time she did not disappear, but circled in silence about one hundred feet away. The gaping bills of two youngsters backed by pairs of large eyes greeted him, asking for food. They were a comical team, all eyes and mouth, bodies covered with dusky down.

Jo constructed a small wickiup of willows in a near-by clump, where, hidden, he could watch the home life. By the middle of June the other three eggs hatched. Five hungry mouths forced the mother into more extended foraging and gave Jo plenty of opportunity to slip into the blind unobserved. Sometimes in returning she passed directly over his head, but so noiselessly that he was not aware of her presence until her shadow slipped ahead.

Just exactly what Nature has in mind when she orders a variation in birthdays among young birds of the same family is a mystery. As Jo watched, it was evident that the first-born had considerable advantage over his younger brothers and sisters. He possessed twice the size, aggressiveness, fighting determination and persistency, enabling him to obtain the largest share of food. So strenuous was his insistence that Mother finally cuffed him out of the nest before the smaller ones could get anything to eat. Aided by her efforts to apportion the food equally, the others obtained a fair share, although the bully usually scrambled back and got more than his portion. This summer, however, it made little difference in their development, for game was plentiful and both parents were clever, industrious hunters.

As the pleasant days passed, Jo saw brought to the nest at different times nearly every variety of small animal found in the vicinity. The male acted as purveyor occasionally, but in a casual and indifferent way. Apparently he forgot for long intervals all domestic duties, and then appeared to remember suddenly and tried to redeem his sins of omission by frequent relays of provender. He seldom helped in dismembering any, just dropped the food and made off. It is possible that Lothario has disciples in the far North.

There were many bird victims, although these were generally large species: small ones were seldom bothered, a pair of snow-buntings raising a family successfully near by. Young ducks predominated in the feathered menu and Jo was fortunate enough to observe, from a knoll overlooking a small pond, the capture of one of these aquatic sacrifices.

A mother Redhead and family (the youngsters well feathered but still unable to fly) were breakfasting in the shallows of this pond. Suddenly all disappeared. The next moment Wapacuthu's gray form hovered above. A head showed. She struck, but only wet her claws. She could see the duck beneath the surface and followed so closely that the swimmer had slight chance to catch a breath. The fourth time the duck rose, it lingered an instant too long at the top, and was seized by the menacing shadow. Wapacuthu did not make the mistake of shifting attack from one to another but pursued the selected one relentlessly until she captured it or the duck reached safety among overhanging branches on the bank.

In looking over some bird books in the factor's scant library Jo learned "Harfang" was one name applied to the snowy owl.

" 'Harfang,' eh? Just fits that overgrown scrapper. I 'm going to tag him!"

He scratched the name on a thin band of brass and after a struggle, during which the fighting imp's claws nicked his hands, Jo succeeded in fastening it loosely on one leg so the growing bone would not be bound.

Henry returned in July and when Jo started south he stopped at the nest.

"Well, so long, you fellers! Maybe I 'll see you again; maybe not. It 's a wide country. As for *you*, Fang, you 'll get along. Keep away from all two-footed animals and some four-footed ones. They 're bad medicine. Don't crowd the rest of 'em like that! They 've as much right there as you have, you overgrown bully!"

The youngsters were fully fledged by the middle of August, but refused to leave home. Why should they? There was always plenty of food, and it was comfortable snuggled down together in the lengthening cool nights. One morning they awoke to find Mother gone; nor did their plaintive squeals recall her with the regulation breakfast. About noon she appeared, a rabbit in her talons, and lit atop Jo's deserted wickiup. The youngsters' pleading cries to bring it nearer were unheeded. She arose, hovered directly above those yawning caverns, wiggled the bait enticingly, went on, dropped the victim fifty feet away. Harfang started for it, half scrambling, half flying, the others trailing. In the ensuing mêlée Bunny's tender flesh was torn to bits, each youngster obtaining a share proportionate to its attacking energy.

Mother's strategy was repeated. The next bait was dropped farther away. By dusk the young owls had traveled some distance from the nest and instead of attempting to return, made themselves fairly comfortable in a willow thicket by burrowing into the deep, soft moss.

Trying his wings next day, Harfang found he could lift his weight; he could *fly!* He celebrated this achievement by fluttering with short wing-beats to one of the previous day's kill, on which he made a fairly satisfactory breakfast.

When Nature accentuates one sense beyond normal, it is usually at expense of the others. She has been generous with owls, giving them a keenness of vision and hearing seldom equaled. With pupils contracted to the size of a pea, the snowy owl endures the glare of the vast Northern wastes of snow and ice, a test which puts a human eye out of commission in a short time. These wonderful organs are further protected by semi-erectile, coarse bristling feathers which keep off the driving snow and enable the snowy to do most of its hunting in daylight.

A tiny squeak issued from the grass far at one side—so distant that nothing but an owl could have heard or located its exact direction. The mouse saw the gray shadow, ran for safety toward its runway, but it was too late: Harfang had it gripped tightly in his needle claws.

The sun's arc narrowed in the south; nights grew longer and colder. From the marshes ducks rose in irregular flocks, mingled, formed in long Vs, and straightened away to the south'ard. Pibroch calls of geese coming from their more Northern home fell on the night air. Most small birds had disappeared weeks before. The sense of restlessness in the atmosphere seized Harfang, so, by easy distances, mainly at night (for he had learned already that daylight traveling was dangerous), he followed, tarrying wherever food was plentiful.

In the early winter he came to a country covered with a network of small streams and lakes. The wide water spaces were frozen, but turbulent brooks were open. His ghostly form, gliding silently along one of these streams, seemed the materialized spirit of the waters. Scarcely pausing in his flight, he swiftly extended one leg, gave it a sudden backward sweep, and with his two front curved claws hooked a fine trout, then the leg automatically bent, throwing in the rear claws. A clever and neat method of fishing!—very different from the clumsy dive of the fish-hawk. Harfang was an artist in piscatorial ways, the fish-hawk a determined craftsman.

The luminous areas, as they became larger and more numerous, the owl avoided, for by daylight he saw these places contained a great number of little boxes filled with two-legged animals. The snow diminished as Harfang moved onward: here were brown fields and gray woods, splashed at intervals by dark groves of evergreen toward which he gravitated naturally; they were like home. Within their thick growth he remained hidden by day, ranging abroad in early morning or late evening for food. Hunting by daylight would have been easier, but it was too risky.

One December night, while winging forward beneath a waning moon, he came to a lake which seemed unbounded. Onward he flew for miles and at last a dim shore-line appeared, apparently snow-covered. Sweeping downward and alighting, he looked around astonished: the ground was white but not cold, and gave easily under his feet! Mice were at play everywhere: he caught half a dozen in as many jumps, found a thick growth of cedars, and turned in. In the morning, from a dune crest, for the first time he surveyed the ocean. That was too large a lake to attempt crossing; he would stay here for a while where rabbits and mice abounded.

A small flock of fish-crows, coursing for clams above the break of surf, discovered and began baiting the marble-like figure.

"Hey, fellers, where did this guy come from?"

"Let 's muss him up a bit!"

"Right-o! Is n't it the 'aughty thing?"

And just there that crowd of dusky freebooters made a serious mistake. They had ballyhooed large-eyed sedate gentlemen before, but the previous victims had been dark-colored and took their berating in stolid silence.

One ventured to thrust its claws at Harfang from behind. That was the last endurable gesture: there was a sudden eruption of great wings, claws, and fierce yellow eyes, and Harfang's talons were driven through the vitals of one of the aggressors. Dropping the inert bunch of sable feathers, he caught another: a terrific constriction of the sharp nippers, and it joined its mate on the ground. The rest dived frantically into the cedars and bayberry bushes.

"Did n't think he could see you in daylight, eh?" remarked a man who had been watching the battle, through glasses, from a bunch of dwarfed evergreens two hundred yards away. "Well, smarties, that was one of the times you-all slipped up! Maybe it will teach you to let the white ones alone. There 's two, though, which 'll never learn."

Toward the latter part of December the belated snow arrived one evening. Harfang, circling the dunes and marshes, was caught in a blinding flurry which came out of the north butt end foremost. He had been close to the southern point of the beach, and when he dropped, seeking the earth, he found instead of the long finger of Monomoy, crested seas whipped white by the rising gale. He tried to beat back, but the wind, already blowing fifty miles an hour, made the effort futile. Headed into the teeth of the roaring air-torrent, again he edged downward, hoping to find solid ground; instead, white-capped waves snarled back at him. He swung off before it through the black night. There was plenty of strength left in the powerful body, when two swaying circles of light shone ahead. Tacking sharply into the wind, Harfang slipped easily over the bulwarks, alighting on the heaving deck almost at the lookout's feet.

A small flock of fish-crows discovered and began baiting the marble-like figure

Exhausted birds seeking shelter were no novelty to the crew of the Nantucket lightship, but never had a visitor like this arrived. The man picked him up, opened the galley door, and put him into a corner. Harfang snapped his bill repeatedly, glared very fiercely, but made no attempt to use his claws.

"Say, Cookie, I got a Christmas turkey for you! Came aboard last night. He is n't exactly a reg'lar turkey, bein' white, but—"

"Where is he?"

Here in the galley. Take a look."

"Turkey, eh? Why, that 's one o' them ghost owls that flies around in snow-storms. What 's he got on his leg? Here, hold these fish-hooks and hold 'em tight while I see! . . . 'Harfang' . . . That 's a funny name! What does it mean?"

"How 'd I know? Sounds like Chinese for 'claws,' to me."

Marooned for months in the winter, those who man these floating outposts of civilization look upon any untoward happening as vastly interesting. Harfang soon became a full-fledged member of the crew and shook down into an unusually docile pet, considering his wild ancestry. At first there was much difference of opinion about his food.

"Naw, he won't eat corned beef. He 's got to have it alive!"

"Well, outside of the bunch that 's mannin' this bucket we have n't got anything alive, not even a mouse. Let 's try him with fish."

The line was baited and a two-pound hake hauled over the side, which had hardly hit the deck before Harfang was straining at the end of his lanyard.

"Ha! That 's the answer!" said the captain. And it certainly was. Catching fresh food for their feathered shipmate was a daily diversion for the boys.

Harfang kept in good condition physically by a "daily dozen" which only a bird could perform. Rising above deck as far as the restraining twine would permit, his great wings moving through a half-circle with extraordinary swiftness, he remained suspended for minutes at a time. He seemed to have the same wing angle control as a humming-bird when poised in one spot. This remarkable exhibition always drew an audience.

"How does he do it without making some noise?" onlookers queried.

The silent action was possible because of the texture of the wing feathers—soft, almost downy; yielding to the air as more rigidly interlocked primaries do not.

April came. The great bird sat for hours on the gunwale, watching wistfully long lines of shearwaters following shifting contours of waves with incredible ease, their stiff wings set at an unvarying right angle. When flocks of scoters appeared, headed north, his uneasiness increased.

"Guess we 'll have to loose the old fellow," said the captain one morning; "he wants to go home."

The restraining lanyard was cast adrift and Harfang swung aloft, free! Then, guided by that mysterious sense of orientation, he headed straight north toward the dwarf alders and willows, for the far land where he was born. Here one morning Jo, trudging across the barren, caught a glint of metal reflecting the early sunlight.

"If that ain't old Harfang! Now, I wonder where you've been all winter!"

www.ingramcontent.com/pod-product-compliance
Lightning Source LLC
Chambersburg PA
CBHW031750080926
51108CB00035B/307
* 9 7 8 1 4 9 3 0 9 7 7 7 7 *